Published for
OXFORD INTERNATIONA
AQA EXAMINATIONS

International A2 Level
BUSINESS

Andrew Gillespie

OXFORD
UNIVERSITY PRESS

OXFORD
UNIVERSITY PRESS

Great Clarendon Street, Oxford, OX2 6DP, United Kingdom
Oxford University Press is a department of the University of
Oxford. It furthers the University's objective of excellence in
research, scholarship, and education by publishing worldwide.
Oxford is a registered trade mark of Oxford University Press in
the UK and in certain other countries

British Library Cataloguing in Publication Data
Data available

978-019-844547-0

10 9

Paper used in the production of this book is a natural,
recyclable product made from wood grown in sustainable
forests. The manufacturing process conforms to the
environmental regulations of the country of origin.

Printed in Great Britain by CPI Group (UK) Ltd.

Acknowledgements
The publishers would like to thank the following for
permissions to use their photographs:

Cover: iStockphoto. All other photos © iStockphoto, except:
p1, 36, 109, 118, 119, 120, 122, 127, 128: Shutterstock

Artwork by QBS Media Services Inc.

Although we have made every effort to trace and contact all
copyright holders before publication this has not been possible
in all cases. If notified, the publisher will rectify any errors or
omissions at the earliest opportunity.

Links to third party websites are provided by Oxford in
good faith and for information only. Oxford disclaims any
responsibility for the materials contained in any third party
website referenced in this work.

Contents

How to use this book

This book fully covers the syllabus for the Oxford AQA International A2 Level Business course (9625). Experienced examiners and teachers have been involved in all aspects of the book, including detailed planning to ensure that the content adheres to the syllabus as closely as possible.

Using this book will ensure that you are well prepared for the assessment at this level, and it gives a solid foundation for further study at university level and beyond. The features below are designed to make learning as interesting and effective as possible.

Activities

These are exercises to do which relate to the chapter content. They can be done in class or as part of individual study.

Progress questions

These are questions through the book to check that you understand the content as you learn. Answers are available in the back of the book.

Key terms

These are the most important vocabulary which you need to learn the definitions of. They are also compiled at the end of the book in a glossary.

Get it right

These are helpful tips and hints to give you the best chance of success.

Link

These are links to other parts of the book for you to find relevant information.

Case study

Subject

These are real-life examples to illustrate the subject matter in the chapters, and are accompanied by questions to test your understanding.

Exam-style questions

These questions are at the end of each chapter section. They use the same command words, structure and marks assignment as the OxfordAQA exams. Answers are available in the back of the book.

The questions, example answers, marks awarded and/or comments that appear in this book were written by the authors. In examinations, the way marks would be awarded to answers like these may be different.

At the end of the book you will find a glossary of the key terms highlighted in bold in the text.

1 Mission, objectives and strategy

This section will develop your knowledge and understanding of:

→ The links between mission, objectives, strategy and the business functions.

→ The need to consider stakeholder needs when making decisions.

Mission

A mission sets out what a business aims to be. An airline may want to be the world's most favourite airline. A hotel may want to be the hotel of choice for families around the world. A mission is often written down as a "mission statement". Examples of mission statements include:

Coca-Cola Company Mission

"Our mission is:

- To refresh the world in mind, body and spirit
- To inspire moments of optimism and happiness through our brands and actions
- To create value and make a difference."

Nike's Mission

"To bring inspiration and innovation to every athlete* in the world.

(*If you have a body you are an athlete.)"

Why does a mission matter?

A mission statement helps employees understand what they are part of and what the organisation is trying to be. The mission helps employees to prioritise and decide how resources should be used. If the business wants to be "a leading innovator" it is clear that a priority is to develop new products and processes. If a business wants to be the customer's first choice, then investment in customer services is a priority.

Producing a mission may be as important as the statement itself. To produce the statement managers may involve employees to help shape the definition of what the business is. If the final statement reflects the views of employees this may help them to feel part of the organisation and more committed to its success.

Objectives

Whilst a mission might set out an overall definition of the organisation it does not provide specific targets. If you want to be the best car company in the world, what does this actually mean? Does this mean you sell the most cars? You have the best safety record? You make the most profit? The general mission needs to be defined in more detail.

An objective is a quantifiable target for the business. A business may have several objectives. For example, the mission may be to "connect the world"; the objectives may be to achieve a 20% market share globally in five years, to launch a new cloud storage system in three years and to increase users of it mobile app by 200,000 by next year. The objectives make it clear exactly what has to be done and when. While the **mission** statement expresses the big picture, the **objective** is more specific than the mission statement. The mission statement is supported by objectives.

An objective should be SMART, this means that it should be:

Specific	It should define exactly what is being measured
Measurable	It should be capable of being measured
Achievable	It should be possible to achieve the target; if the target is not realistic then employees will not be committed to them
Relevant	It should be clear to everyone involved why the objective should be aimed for; understanding why motivates people to want to achieve their goals and understand the bigger picture
Time specific	It should be clear when an objective needs to be achieved; this enables managers to plan properly for them

MISSION ⟶ OBJECTIVES

▲ Figure 1.1: The mission statement is supported by objectives

Key terms

A **mission** sets out why a business exists.

An **objective** is a quantifiable target.

Get it right

When deciding whether a business is successful or whether a plan worked it is important to consider the business mission and objectives. You can only judge if something is successful if you know what it was trying to achieve; success should be measured against this.

Case study

Our Credo (this means "What we believe" and is Johnson and Johnson's name for its mission statement)

The statement below sets out the mission of Johnson and Johnson, a healthcare business operating in 60 countries around the world with over 134,000 employees:

"We believe our first responsibility is to the patients, doctors and nurses, to mothers and fathers and all others who use our products and services. In meeting their needs everything we do must be of high quality. We must constantly strive to provide value, reduce our costs and maintain reasonable prices. Customers' orders must be serviced promptly and accurately. Our business partners must have an opportunity to make a fair profit.

We are responsible to our employees who work with us throughout the world. We must provide an inclusive work environment where each person must be considered as an individual. We must respect their diversity and dignity and recognize their merit. They must have a sense of security, fulfillment and purpose in their jobs. Compensation must be fair and adequate and working conditions clean, orderly and safe. We must support the health and well-being of our employees and help them fulfill their family and other personal responsibilities. Employees must feel free to make suggestions and complaints. There must

be equal opportunity for employment, development and advancement for those qualified. We must provide highly capable leaders and their actions must be just and ethical.

We are responsible to the communities in which we live and work and to the world community as well. We must help people be healthier by supporting better access and care in more places around the world. We must be good citizens — support good works and charities, better health and education, and bear our fair share of taxes. We must maintain in good order the property we are privileged to use, protecting the environment and natural resources.

Our final responsibility is to our stockholders. Business must make a sound profit. We must experiment with new ideas. Research must be carried on, innovative programs developed, investments made for the future and mistakes paid for. New equipment must be purchased, new facilities provided and new products launched. Reserves must be created to provide for adverse times. When we operate according to these principles, the stockholders should realize a fair return."

www.jnj.com/credo/

1 Explain two factors that might influence the mission of Johnson and Johnson.
2 Analyse the potential benefits to Johnson and Johnson of producing a mission statement.

Typical business objectives

Managers may set a number of different objectives for their business. These may include:

- **Profit objectives:** Profit measures the extent to which revenue is greater than costs. This profit shows that the business is adding value through its activities. Profit is common measure of the success of managers. Profit is an internal source of finance which means that it can fund investment (as opposed to the company having to raise money externally through loans).

- **Cash flow:** Simply making a profit may not be enough; it may also be important to focus on the timings of payments. Imagine for example that many sales are on credit. This would count as revenue because the sales have occurred but the cash has not yet come in and so cash flow could be a problem. Managers may need to ensure the payment terms from customers and to suppliers are suitable to ensure the cash flow is acceptable.

- **Shareholder value:** A company is owned by its shareholders. Shareholders will want the managers to earn more because that way the owners will be happy with the way the business is being run. The shareholders will be interested in:
    - the share price – the higher the share price the greater the value of what investors own
    - the dividends paid; this is the financial payment to shareholders that usually occurs each year. The shareholders vote on the recommendations of the managers.

- **Growth:** Managers may want the business to grow. This shows they are being successful in making the business bigger, which is good for their own success. It may also make the business more powerful and a more well-known brand.

- A business may also have social objectives. These are targets set to improve society, investing in the local community to improve the quality of life and helping certain groups in society, e.g. employing those who have been in prison.

- A business might also have environmental objectives. For example, a business might aim to:
    - reduce the pollution from its factories
    - recycle to reduce waste.

Short termism vs long termism

Short termism occurs when managers focus on short-term objectives. Long termism occurs when managers plan for many years ahead. If managers take a long-term approach they are more likely to:

- Invest in training staff.
- Invest in new equipment.
- Invest in research and development of new products and new processes.

If managers have a short-term focus they will concentrate on activities that bring returns quickly. They will not consider activities that will take many years to earn returns.

Link

For more about cash flow, see Chapter 5 in the AS book.

The causes of short termism are:

- The pressure on managers from investors to generate returns quickly. This may be the case if shareholders are looking for the highest possible returns they can get and insist that managers deliver them. This is most likely in a public limited company where many investors may be looking for short-term financial rewards. The owners of public limited businesses are often other companies such as banks and pensions funds; these investors need to earn a return for their owners and so are looking for high dividends and/or share price increases. Managers of public limited companies may be forced therefore to find ways of boosting short-term rewards to investors.

- The desire by managers to achieve short-term gains. Many managers will be looking to do well in their job and to get promoted. They are often intending to move jobs within a few years and so want to achieve short-term gains. They will be less interested in very long-term projects because they may not be there to take the credit.

The effects of short termism

Short termism means that managers focus on project that bring quick returns and are less interested in projects that might be better for the business but take longer to be successful.

This may mean with short termism:

- Less money is allocated to areas such research and development and training.
- There is less interest in training staff.
- There will be a strong focus on having a relatively short payback period for investments.
- There is little investment in building the long-term brand.

Strategy

A **strategy** is a long-term plan. It sets out how an objective is going to be achieved. For example, a business may want to increase profits over the next two years but it could do this in different ways. It could focus on developing and launching new products. It could target new countries. It could target new customer groups. It could focus on reducing costs.

All of these are different strategies.

A strategic decision usually involves:

- High levels of investment.
- A long-term commitment of resources.
- High levels of risk.

A mission sets out the overall purpose of a business. The objectives set specific targets. The strategy sets out how the diagram will be achieved.

> **Key term**
>
> A **strategy** is a long-term plan of action to achieve an objective.

Activity

Research the news and identify a strategic decision that a business has made, for example, a business buying another business, launching a new type of product, entering a new market or introducing ways of cutting costs. With reference to the features of a strategy described above, explain why you believe this is a strategic decision.

Get it right

When considering the impact of a decision on a business you should think about the effect on the different functions of marketing, HR, operations and finance. You might also consider the interrelationship between these functions; you only want to generate more sales if have the capacity to produce and if you can do so in a way that it is profitable.

Link

You can read in more detail about the activities of the different functions in the AS book Chapter 3.

▲ Figure 1.1: How the Mission, Objective and Strategy are linked

Business functions

The functions of a business are:

- **Marketing:** these activities deal with the interaction between the business and its customers.
- **Operations:** these activities are responsible for the development and delivery of the product or service. This includes research and development activity, IT and logistics.
- **Finance:** these activities are responsible for raising finance, deciding how it is used and measuring the profits of the business.
- **Human resources:** these activities are responsible for the acquisition, retention, rewarding and development of people within the organisation.

Strategy and functions

Strategic decisions will have implications for the business functions. For example, if the business decides to enter a new market this will involve new marketing activities. For example, the promotion of the product may be changed and new distribution channels may be required; new employees may need to be recruited in different regions and managers will have to consider what are suitable rewards.

Having decided the overall objectives for the business (sometimes called corporate objectives) and the strategy to achieve these, managers will set objectives in their functional areas,

For example:

- **Mission:** become a global business.
- **Corporate objective:** achieve sales of $10 million in China in five years.
- **Strategy:** sell products in China.
- **Operational objectives:** establish production facilities in China in two years.
- **Marketing objectives:** develop a marketing plan and launch campaign for two years.
- **Human resource objectives:** recruit staff for the Chinese project now and for Chinese production facility in two years.
- **Financial objectives:** establish budgeting systems.

This section will develop your knowledge and understanding of:

→ The use and value of SWOT (strengths, weaknesses opportunities, threats) analysis.

To decide on the best strategy to achieve an objective, managers will assess the environment in which their businesses operate. They will look for positive developments that create opportunities for them and other changes that might create a threat for their business. The extent to which changes create an opportunity or a threat depends on the position of the business and its strengths and weaknesses. If, for example, a business is good at entering international markets and changes in trade agreements open up new markets this represents an opportunity; this would not be the case if the business was not good at entering overseas markets. If a business has high levels of debt then an increase in interest rate might be a threat; however, it would be less of an issue if there were not high levels of borrowing.

SWOT analysis involves an analysis of the:

- Strengths of the current position of the business.
- Weaknesses of the current position of the business.
- Opportunities for the business.
- Threats facing the businesses.

The strengths and weaknesses of a business refer to its internal position; what is happening within the business. The opportunities and threats are external to the business; they represent changes happening outside of the business itself.

SWOT analysis needs to be conducted regularly as conditions change. SWOT analysis can help select a strategy but managers must then implement it effectively.

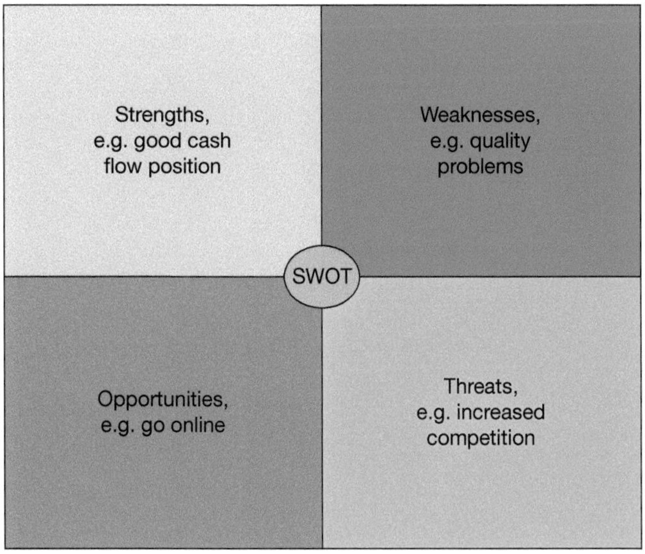

> **Key term**
>
> **SWOT analysis:** an examination of the strengths and weaknesses (internal) a business has and the opportunities and threats (external) it faces.

> **Link**
>
> Part of SWOT analysis will include an assessment of the finances of the business. The financial position of a business can be analysed using ratio analysis. See Chapter 3.

▲ Figure 1.2: A SWOT analysis

This section will develop your knowledge and understanding of:

→ The need to consider stakeholder needs when making decisions.

Stakeholders

Stakeholders are any individuals or groups that are affected by the activities of a business. Imagine a big city shopping centre. The stores in the centre will have employees and owners and they will be affected by how well the businesses do. For employees the success of the business will affect if they have a job and the amount they are likely to earn. For the owners it will affect the profits of the business and their rewards on their investment. The success of one business will also affect the success of others. If one restaurant in the shopping centre does particularly well it may take customers away from other restaurants there. On the other hand the success of the restaurant may bring customers to the shopping centre and increase sales of other types of stores.

The success of the shops in the shopping centre will also affect other **stakeholders** such as:

- The local and national government. The businesses at the centre are likely to pay local and or national taxes. This will generate revenue for the government. They will also be expected to follow local and national laws. For example, this might affect when they open and what they are allowed to sell.
- The local community. The community around the centre will be affect by any congestion that is caused as people drive to shop there and ark their vehicles. Any litter and waste that is created by shoppers and the shops themselves may also affect the community.

> **Key term**
>
> **Stakeholder**: an individual or group who has an interest in a business. They can be affected by a business decision and/or have their views considered as part of the decision.

▲ Figure 1.3: Examples of different stakeholders of a business

Progress questions

1   State three stakeholders of your school or college.
2   "A stakeholder is always a shareholder". True or false?
    Explain your answer.

Activity

Choose a business you know and identify the different stakeholders affected by its actions.

Stakeholder mapping

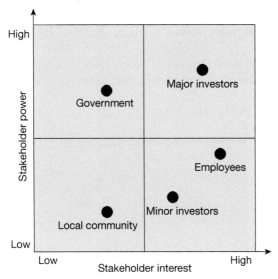

▲ Figure 1.4: An example of a stakeholder map

When making decisions managers may want to classify their stakeholders. This process is known as "**stakeholder mapping**". Stakeholder mapping categorises stakeholders according to their power and their interest in the business. In Figure 1.4, the shareholders have a high level of interest and power. This is typical of many companies because shareholders will want to know what is happening in the business and will influence who the managers are. In this example the government is not particularly interested but is powerful because it can pass laws that affect the business. How interested the government is may depend on what sort of business it is (for example, it will be interested in manufacturers of defence equipment or large businesses that employ hundreds of thousands of people). Employees are shown as interested (because decisions affect their pay and job security) but not powerful. However, groups of employees arguing together can be more powerful than individuals. In this example the local community are not very interested or powerful, but this will depend on what the business does, for example, is the business creating congestion in the area? The position of different groups will vary from business to business and over time. For example, if a business was criticised for safety issues the level of government interest may increase. This means that stakeholder mapping is not a one-off activity.

Managers may treat the different stakeholders differently according to the category they are in.

- **Low interest, low power:** These stakeholders have little connection with the business and managers will not need to spend much time worrying about them.

Key term

A **stakeholder map** categorises stakeholders in terms of their level of interest and their level of power.

Activity

Go back to your list of stakeholders for a business you know. Plot where four of these groups fit on a stakeholder map. Explain why you have placed them in the positions you have.

- **High interest, high power:** These are very significant stakeholders. They care about what is happening in the business and they are able to influence the decisions as they have power. Managers will want to ensure these stakeholders are kept well informed and are listened to when making decisions.
- **High interest, low power:** These stakeholders are interested in what happens in the business but are not in a position to actually influence what is done. Managers may keep them informed but are not particularly concerned about what they think or do.
- **Low interest, high power:** These stakeholders have a great deal of influence but are not especially concerned about this business. Managers will want them to be happy with what is happening but they will not need regular communication as they are not that interested.

Using the stakeholder map

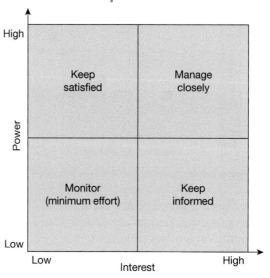

▲ **Figure 1.5:** How managers might treat different stakeholders

By identifying the relative power and interest of a stakeholder managers can decide on the most appropriate way of dealing with that individual or group. Resources are always limited and therefore need to be used most effectively.

For example, managers will:

- Make little effort to communicate or please stakeholders that have little interest in the business and little power.
- Keep stakeholders who are very interested in the business but not very powerful informed about what is happening but not offer much else.
- Keep groups that are powerful but who have little interest in the business satisfied with what the business does; managers won't particularly want these stakeholders to become interested.
- Pay a lot of attention to stakeholders who are powerful and interested and manage these critical relationships.

Progress question

3 How might stakeholder mapping be useful to managers?

Stakeholder objectives

The typical objectives of stakeholders are shown in the table below:

▼ Table 1.1: Typical objectives of stakeholders

Stakeholder groups	Typical objectives
Employees	Employment, good earnings, good working conditions
Owners	Profits, higher dividends and an increase in the value of the business
Customer	Good quality, value for money
Suppliers	Regular orders, payment on time
Community	Support of local community
Government	Payment of taxes, act in legal manner

Do stakeholders' objectives coincide or clash?

At times the objectives of stakeholders may coincide; different groups may be working together towards the same targets. For example, if a business provides better quality products this might help sales and profits; this might then lead to more jobs and wages for employees and more rewards to the owners. More sales may mean more orders and profits for suppliers and more money circulating in the local and national community. Several groups can gain at the same time from more profits.

However, this may not always be the case; at times the objectives of stakeholders may clash. Paying employees higher earnings may reduce profits for investors. Paying suppliers on time may weaken the cashflow position of the business and reduced its value. Greater taxes for the government may mean lower profits for investors. Managers will be constantly balancing different demands from different stakeholders to find the best course of action.

Progress questions

4   "A strategy is a quantifiable target." True or false?
5   What is SWOT analysis?
6   Identify three stakeholders in a business.
7   State the axes used on a stakeholder map.
8   State two possible objectives of a business.

Activities

Go back to your list of stakeholders of the business you know.

1   Think of two instances where there may be a conflict of interests between different groups.
2   Identify two instances where the interests of different groups may coincide.

Get it right

When writing about stakeholders you rarely need to consider every group. In any situation some stakeholders may be more important than others. Focus on the key groups in any situation.

Exam-style questions

Explanation and analysis

1   Explain one benefit to a large business of having a clear objective.   (4 marks)

2   Explain one benefit of stakeholder mapping when changing strategy.   (4 marks)

3   Explain two ways a stakeholder groups might be affected by a decision to invest
    in new technology.   (6 marks)

4   Analyse how a focus on short termism might affect two of the functional areas
    of a business.   (9 marks)

5   Analyse how SWOT analysis helps a business to change strategy effectively.   (9 marks)

Evaluation

6   You have just become Chief Executive of a multinational that has been performing badly.
    Do you think it is a priority to review the mission statement? Assess the arguments for
    and against and make a judgement.   (12 marks)

7   You want to change the strategy of your business. Do you think you should involve
    stakeholders in developing this strategy? Assess the arguments for and against and
    make a judgement.   (12 marks)

2 Analysing the existing internal position of a business

This section will develop your knowledge and understanding of:

→ Assessing the financial performance of a business using statements of financial position, income statements and financial ratios.

Key terms

A **statement of financial position** is the financial document that lists all the assets and liabilities of a business on a specified date.

An **income (or profit and loss) statement** is a document that gives the revenues (i.e. income) and costs for a business and the resulting profit or loss for a stated time period.

Profit: measures the difference between revenue and costs.

Part of analysing the existing position of a business will include an assessment of its financial position. If you are working for a business you will have access to internal data. If you are analysing a business you do not work for you will have to use their published accounts. The published accounts include a statement of what it owns and what it owes at a particular moment in time; this is called a **statement of financial position**. It also includes a statement showing its revenue, costs and **profits** over a year; this is called the **income statement** (or it is sometimes called the profit and loss statement). Using these financial statements it is possible to undertake financial ratio analysis.

Progress question

1   Why do you think it is necessary to examine the balance sheet and the profit and loss statement of a business?

Profit for the year

The profit of a business measures the difference between the value of its sales and the costs of producing marketing and making those sales.

The profit for the year is calculated using:

Revenue (also called turnover): this measures the value of sales

Minus

Cost of goods sold: this measures the costs of producing the items sold

---

= Gross profit

Minus

Expenses: these are overheads of the business such as marketing and administrative costs

---

= Operating profit

Plus

Interest and earnings from investments

Minus

Interest paid on borrowings

Taxes

= Profit for the year

The profit for the year is a common measure of the financial performance of a business. It shows the excess earned from selling the products in terms of the earnings for the year.

Financial ratios

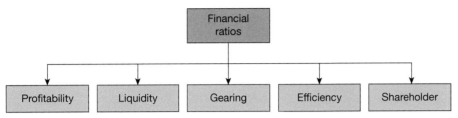

▲ Figure 2.1: Types of financial ratios

An analyst will usually be interested in measures of:

- **Profitability:** is the profit good relative to the level of sales and the long-term funds of the business? The profit is measured in $ and shows the amount by which revenue exceeds costs. Profitability measures how big the profit is in relation to the sales or long-term funds of the business. This is important because it gives us a sense of scale. $1 million dollars profit may seem like a large amount but if this was the profit of a business the scale of Microsoft this would give a low profitability ratio and would not be impressive.

- **Liquidity:** these measures will assess the ability of the business to pay what it owes in the short term. Liquidity is measured by considering what the business own can turn into cash quickly (called current assets) compared to what it owes and has to pay out in the next year(called current liabilities).

- **Gearing:** this assesses the way in which the business raises its long-term funds; what proportion of borrowed compared to the proportion from investors and profits. By analysing gearing an analyst is considering not just how much money the business has but how it got it and the implications of this.

- **Efficiency:** these ratios measure how efficiently resources are used; for example, whether the business has too much or too little inventory; whether it is owed too much money by customers.

- **Shareholder ratios:** these measure the rewards received by investors and enable analysts to consider how good these are relative to other investments.

Progress questions

2 Name three stakeholder groups that might be interested in the financial performance of a particular business.

3 Why is it important to measure profitability not just profit?

Profitability ratios
Profit margin
The **profit margin** shows the profits of a business relative to its revenue. If the profit margin is 1% this means out of every dollar of revenue received 1 cent is profit, if the profit margin is 5% then out

Key term

Profit margin: measures the profit as a percentage of the sales.

of every dollar received as revenue 5 cents is profit. In one sense a high margin is desirable because it means more profit is earned out of every dollar. However, it is important to consider the strategy of the business. Some businesses aim to have a low profit margin but high sales; the high level of sales compensates for the small profit made per dollar and overall high profits can still be made. On the other hand, some businesses may have relatively low sales overall and so aim to make a high profit margin on each sale.

There are different types of profit margin because there are different types of profits. For example you might analyse the:

Gross profit margin. This is measured by the equation:

(gross profits/sales) × 100

Or

Operating profit margin. This is measured by the equation: (operating profit/sales) × 100

Managers will consider how these are changing over time and why differences occur. They will compare their margins with competitor businesses. They will also consider the difference between gross and profit margins to gain an insight into business performance. If the gross profit margin is relatively high but the operating profit margin is relatively low, for example this suggests that the overheads of the business may need controlling more closely.

Return on capital employed (ROCE)

This is a key **profitability ratio**. The **capital employed** is the total long-term funds in the business. It is made up of:

- Funds raised from selling shares.
- Funds from retained profits.
- Funds from long-term borrowing.

The managers have these long-term funds and use them to run the business and generate a profit. The **return on capital employed (ROCE)** measures how much profit has been generated from this capital employed as a percentage. If the ROCE is 10% this means that the profits earned over a year are 10% of the long-term funds. If the ROCE is 15% this means the profits earned over a year are 15% of the long-term funds in the business. All things being equal, owners and managers would want the ROCE to be as high as possible because it would show that the funds of the business are being used effectively to generate profit.

The ROCE will depend on:

- The value of the sales generated from the capital employed.
- The profit margin on each sale.

To increase the ROCE, therefore, a business may:

- Increase its sales given the capital employed it has.
- Increase the profit margin on its sales.

Key terms

Profitability ratios: a means of measuring different types of profit in relation to sales revenue or capital employed.

Gross profit margin: the relationship between the gross profit and the sales revenue of a business.

Return on capital employed: measures profit relative to the capital employed as a percentage.

Capital employed: the total value of all share capital and retained profits and loans of a business.

4   How can a business that has a low operating profit margin earn a high
    return on capital employed?

Liquidity

Liquidity is a measure of a business's ability to pay its short-term
debts. It is essential that a business is able to meet any short-term
financial obligations if it wants to continue to trade. The liquidity ratio
will provide more information about the extent of the current assets of
a business relative to its current liabilities.

At any moment a business will have assets that are in the form of cash
(which means they are very liquid) or are expected to be turned into
cash within the next 12 months.

These "liquid" assets include:

- Money owed to the business by customers (this is called
  receivables).
- Inventory (these are items that will be used up in production or
  will be sold) which used to be called "stock".
- Cash and money in the bank.

The assets that are expected to be turned into cash within 12 months
are called "**current assets**".

The business will also have money that is owed. The money owed
to others that has to be paid within the next 12 months is called
"**current liabilities**".

Current liabilities include:

- Money owed to suppliers (this is called payables).
- An overdraft.
- Tax that has to be paid.
- Interest that has to be paid on loans.

The liquidity of a business can be measured using the current ratio.

Current ratio

The **current ratio** measures: Current assets: current liabilities

For example: if current assets are $40,000 and current liabilities are
$20,000 this means the business can pay off the money it owes over
the next 12 months two times over. The current ratio is 2 (or this is
sometimes written as 2:1)

If, however, the current assets were $10,000 and the current liabilities
were $20,000 this would mean the current assets were only 0.5 of the
current liabilities. The business does not have the short-term assets
it needs to pay off what it owes over the next 12 months. This might
suggest it has a liquidity problem. In general if the current ratio is low
(for example less than 1) this may suggest liquidity problem. Given
that some of the inventory may not be easy to sell some analysts
would start to worry if the current ratio is below 1.5.

Progress questions

5   The current assets of a business are $12 million. The current liabilities are $8 million. Calculate the current ratio.

6   Why might a business not want the current ratio to be too high?

7   Why might a business not want the current ratio to be too low?

However, as with all analysis, it is important to think about the context.

Imagine the current ratio is low but the business is a huge multinational company. Although the current ratio may suggest there could be problems paying the bills in reality the business could:

- Get a loan if required.
- Negotiate with suppliers so they did not insist on payment this year.
- Sell other assets such as land if needs to be to pay the bills.

Whilst analysts usually worry if the current ratio is too low they may also be concerned if it is too high. If the current assets are very high compared to the liabilities this may be because of high levels of cash, inventory or receivables. All of these could be a concern because:

- Cash does not earn a return; there is therefore an opportunity cost of holding cash – the money could be better used elsewhere.
- Inventory may not sell; a business may stockpile inventory only to find it goes out of fashion or demand patterns change.
- Receivables may not be paid. Too much money in the form of receivables may create a risk.

Gearing

As we saw earlier the capital employed is made up of:

- Funds raised from selling shares.
- Funds from retained profits.
- Funds from long-term borrowing (called non-current liabilities).

Analysts will be interested in the exact composition of the capital employed. In particular they will want to know what proportion of it is borrowed; this is known as gearing.

Example 1:

Non-current liabilities $10 million

Issued share capital $25 million

Retained profit $5 million

Capital employed = $10 million +$25 million + $5 million = $40 million

Gearing = (non-current liabilities/capital employed) × 100 = ($10/$40) × 100 = 25%

Example 2:

Non-current liabilities $80 million

Issued share capital $35 million

Retained profit $5 million

Capital employed = $80 million +$35 million + $5 million = $120 million

Gearing = (non-current liabilities/capital employed) × 100
= ($80/$120) × 100 = 75%

High gearing means that a high proportion of the capital employed is borrowed. This means a high percentage of the long-term funds of the business are in the form of loans.

Low gearing means that a low proportion if its long-term funds is borrowed. The majority must have been raised through selling shares or through retained profits.

High gearing may be a concern because of the interest payments on the loans. The high interest payments may be a burden on the business, especially if profits are low. With low profits the business may struggle to meet the interest payments. On the other hand if profits are high then the interest payments can be met easily, which should leave relatively high funds in the form of profits for investors.

Of course, the question remains – what is "high" gearing? As ever it depends on the context. In general, analysts begin to worry about interest payments if gearing is above 50% of the capital employed. However, it depends on:

- The interest rates; if they are fixed at a low rate it may make sense to have high gearing.
- The profits of the business; if profits are high then the interest payments may not be concerned.

Gearing in itself is not a problem. It often makes commercial sense to borrow to go ahead with a project which then generates profits and repays the loan relatively easily. The problems occur when profits are too low and the interest payments become a problem.

> **Key term**
>
> **Gearing ratio:** measures the percentage of the capital of a company that is from fixed interest-bearing sources:
>
> **High gearing:** a high proportion of the capital employed is borrowed.
>
> **Low gearing:** a low proportion of the capital employed is borrowed.

> **Progress questions**
>
> 8 If the capital employed of a business is $40 million and the long-term borrowing is $5 million what is the gearing? What if it borrowed an additional $3 million?
>
> 9 Explain why a business may not want its gearing ratio to be too high.
>
> 10 Explain why a business may not want its gearing ratio to be too low.

Efficiency ratios

These measure how efficiently resources are being used by managers. They include payables days, receivables days and inventory turnover.

Payables days

This measures how much is owed to suppliers in terms of the days' worth of purchases. If, for example, a business spends $10,000 a year on purchasing resources and at any moment owes $5,000 this means it owes the equivalent of half of a year's sales. This could be presented as payables of six months or in terms of days half a year would be 182.5 days.

To calculate the payables we use the equation:

$$\frac{\text{Payables}}{\text{Cost of sales}} \times 365$$

For example, $\frac{\$5,000}{\$10,000} \times 365 = 0.5 \times 365 = 182.5$ days

Managers may be concerned if the **payables day** is too low because they might think they should bargain harder to get longer times to pay suppliers.

Receivables days

This measures how much is owed to a business in terms of the equivalent days' worth of sales. For example, if a business sells $500,000 sales in a year and at any moment is owed $50,000 by customers, this is equal to one tenth of a year's sales, One tenth of a year is $0.1 \times 365 = 36.5$ days' worth of sales.

Managers might be concerned if the **receivables days** ratio was too high as it might suggest that the business was not collecting the money it was owed very effectively. Having said this, giving customers more credit may be a deliberate activity to promote more sales; customers might be more willing to buy a product if they have longer to pay.

To calculate the payables we use the equation:

$$\frac{\text{Receivables}}{\text{Sales}} \times 365$$

For example:

$\frac{\$50,000}{\$500,000} \times 365 = 0.1 \times 365 = 36.5$ days' worth of sales.

Inventory turnover

This measures how much inventory the business holds relative to how much it sells in a year, For example, if a business typically sells $20,000 of goods a year and at any given moment is holding $5,000 of inventory this means the inventory it has would be "turned over" or replaced four times in a year.

To calculate the **inventory turnover**, we use the equation

$$\frac{\text{Cost of sales}}{\text{Inventory}}$$

For example, if the cost of sales are $20,000 and inventory is $5,000 the inventory turnover is:

$20,000/\$5,000 = 4$ times.

The appropriate rate of inventory turnover will depend on the context. If a business is adopting a just-in-time approach, for example, this means that it would expect a relatively high inventory turnover as it would hold relatively little inventory at any moment and replace it regularly.

If, however, a business sold elite sports cars, the amount of inventory it held might be relatively high and it might not expect to replace this inventory many times in a year.

Key terms

Payable days: measures how much is owed by the business in terms of days of sales.

Receivables days: measures how much is owed to the business in terms of days of sales.

Inventory turnover: measures how often inventory is replaced in a year.

Ratio: one thing measured in terms of another.

When considering the values of the **efficiency ratios** it is important for managers to:

- Look at the trends over time to analyse what is changing and why. A decline in profit margins year on year may be more significant than a one off fall.
- Look at competitors' ratios to compare performance; if you have an inventory turnover of 4 but rivals have 6 it may mean they are holding less inventory at any moment; there may be something to learn about inventory control.
- Consider the context – for example, the types of product involved and the objectives of the business. For example, is the receivables figure deliberately high because the business is offering credit to boost sales?

Progress question

11 Why might a business not want its inventory turnover to be too low?

Key terms

Efficiency ratios: measure how efficiently resources are used in the business

Dividend per share: the rate of return that a holder of ordinary shares receives for each share held.

Dividend yield: measures the dividend per share as a percentage of the share price.

Price/earnings ratio: shows the relationship between the earnings per share and the market price of the share.

Shareholder ratios

If you invest in a business you will be interested in:

- What happens to the share price. If the share price of a company increases you could sell your shares and make a financial gain.
- The amount paid out each year. The amount paid out is called the "dividends". This is the income of the shareholders – dividends create a return for shareholders. Shareholders will be interested in the dividends paid on each share (the dividends per share) and how much this is relative to the share price as a percentage (this is called the dividend yield).

Dividend per share

Dividend per share = total dividends / total number of shares

e.g. total dividends paid $10,000; total number of shares is 50,000

Dividend per share = $10,000/50,000 = $0.20 = 20 cents per share

Dividend yield

Dividend yield = (dividend per share/ market share price) × 100

e.g. dividend per share = $0.20. Current market share price = $2.00

Dividend yield = ($0.20/$2.00) × 100 = 10%.

The higher the dividend yield the greater the returns from dividends are for the investors relative to the price of buying a share.

Managers will recommend the dividend to be paid out; this will be voted on by the owners. Paying out more dividends means the owners earn more now; however, this leaves less funds in the business for investment which may be bad for its long-term profits and the share price.

Price earnings ratio

The **price/earnings ratio (P/E ratio)** measures the current price of a share to the earnings of the share. The earnings are the profits of the company divided up per share. If a company has $400,000 profits and

800,000 shares the earnings per share would be $400,000/800,000 = $0.50. The dividend per share is what is actually paid out per share; the earnings per share is what could be paid out if all the profits are distributed.

The P/E ratio shows how much investors are paying for a share compared to the profits earned by the company. If investors are confident about the company demand for shares will increase and this will pull up the price; this increases the P/E ratio. If, however, there was a loss of confidence in the business the share priced would fall bringing down the P/E ratio.

The P/E ratio is therefore an indication of the value of the business relative to its profits. If it is low the shares may be relatively cheap to buy; the question is why that is. If the P/E ratio is high it suggests the company is highly valued at the moment.

Progress question

12 Explain one reason why the P/E ratio of a company may be high.

▼ **Table 2.1**: Summary of ratios

Ratio	Ratio	Equation	
Profitability	Profit margin	$\dfrac{\text{Profit}}{\text{Sales}} \times 100\%$	
	Return on capital employed	$\dfrac{\text{Profit}}{\text{Capital employed}} \times 100\%$	Generally a high return is desired
Liquidity	Current ratio	$\dfrac{\text{Current assets}}{\text{Current liabilities}}$	If less than 1.5 it may suggest liquidity issues (but it depends)
Gearing	Gearing	$\dfrac{\text{Non-current liabilities}}{\text{Capital employed}} \times 100\%$	If over 50% may be too high (but it depends)
Shareholder	Dividend per share	Total dividends/total number of shares= cents	No "typical" number
	Dividend yield	$\dfrac{\text{Dividend per share}}{\text{Share price}} \times 100\%$	Often around 3% to 5% but it depends
	Price/earnings ratio	$\dfrac{\text{Share profit}}{\text{Profit per share}}$	Varies

Who uses financial ratios?

There will be many different stakeholder groups who will look at the financial ratios. Each group may have a particular focus. For example:

- **Shareholders:** they will be interested in the dividend yield to see the return they get on the shares they have bought. They will also be interested in other key ratios as these are likely to affect share price. The return in capital employed is a measure of how well managers are using the finds they have to generate profits; if this is poor this may reduce the share price.

- **Potential suppliers:** they may be particularly interested in the liquidity position of the business – can it pay its bills? If the liquidity position is poor suppliers may be wary of accepting a contract from the business.

The limitations of financial ratios

Financial ratios can provide an insight into the position of a business and can highlight the actions managers may want to take.

However, ratio analysis has limitations:

- It does not include the context; managers need to be aware of the context in which the ratios are calculated. For example, a ROCE of 8% may be low if markets are growing and demand is booming but may be high if generally demand is low. A profit margin of 10% may be low for a business selling sports cars but high for a food retailer.
- It does not include qualitative factors. A business that is focusing on social objectives may not be so concerned by a low ROCE as one that is focused on profits.
- It does not show the future strategy of the business. Most ratios are backward looking and show what has happened. Stakeholders will generally be interested in what is going to happen.

Window dressing

Window dressing occurs when managers or their accountants interpret accounting policies to make their financial statements look as good as possible.

For example:

- In some countries it is possible to include a value of your brands when you are listing the assets of the business. This will increase the value of the business' assets. The problem is that there is no simple way of assessing the value of a brand and so accountants may adopt a way that gives a particularly high value.
- When valuing the inventory of a business managers should consider if they can actually sell it or not; if they are going to struggle to sell it this should be reflected in how much it is valued at. Managers may take a positive view of the likelihood that the inventory will be sold, which means assets are valued too highly.

Profit centres

Profit centres are parts of a business (such as a department, division or outlet) for which profits are measured.

Profit centres are used to identify the profits of different parts of the business. For example:

- A retailer may be interested in the profits of different stores or regions.
- A business may be interested in the profits of different products.

To calculate the profits of a profit centre managers must:

- Identify the revenue of this centre, e.g. how much revenue is generated by a particular store.
- Identify the costs that belong directly to each centre, e.g. the costs of staff that work there, the costs of materials only used in each one.

Activities

1. Research a company of your choice.

2. Look at its accounts in its most recent annual report.

Calculate the following ratios:

- Profit margin
- Return on capital employed
- Current ratio
- Gearing
- Dividend per share
- Dividend yield

To what extent do you think the business is in a good financial position?

Key terms

Window dressing: changes made in the accounts of a business in order to present a more favourable picture to the users of the accounts, e.g. assets such as "goodwill" are overstated to make the business look better than it is.

A **profit centre** is a part of the business for which revenues and costs and profits are measured.

- Allocate costs that belong to the business as a whole. For example, senior management's salaries belong to the overall business and so a decision must be made on how best to allocate these costs between different stores or regions or products. The allocation of these costs which do not directly belong to a centre (and so are called indirect costs) may be based on factors such as the number of staff, the sales revenue or even the floorspace (in the case of stores). Different methods will give different allocations.

Profit centres are important because they can highlight what is happening to profits of part of the business within the overall profits of the whole business. It may, for example, that some parts of the business are much more profitable than others. Managers may want to know why and see if the other parts can learn from the more profitable sections. In some cases managers may want to shut down the less profitable parts of the business; however, when doing this it is important to remember that the indirect costs allocated to this section will still exist and must now be reallocated to the remaining parts.

Progress questions

13 How might a business benefit from introducing profit centres?

14 How might a business benefit from analysing the performance of its profit centres?

This section will develop your knowledge and understanding of:

→ How to analyse data other than financial data to assess the strengths and weaknesses of a business.

Financial data can provide invaluable insights into areas such as the cashflow of the business, the profitability of different product lines and the overall returns being generated. However, managers will want to analyse each of the functional areas of the business to ensure that resources are being used efficiently and effectively.

For example, in marketing, managers will consider issues such as:

- The current and forecasted sales of the business and the market share this represents.
- The product portfolio (using the Boston matrix) and the actions that may need to be taken to achieve a balanced portfolio.
- The market trends in terms of overall market growth and the growth or decline of different market segments.
- The position of a product in its product life cycle and the actions that may need to be taken, such as extension strategies.
- The current marketing mix and how this may need to be developed in future – for example, whether there is a greater need for digital marketing.
- The size and allocation of the marketing budget.

In operations, managers will consider issues such as:

- The current capacity utilisation and the capacity required for the future.
- The performance of the business in terms of different operational objectives such as quality, speed of response, flexibility, dependability and unit costs.
- The environmental impact of operational decisions.
- The current and future suppliers and the management of the supply chain.
- The production locations and the use of offshoring and subcontractors.
- The use of technology.

In human resources, managers will consider issues such as:

- The motivation and engagement of employees.
- The numbers and skills the business has and will need in the future.
- The training required.
- The productivity of employees.
- Labour costs as a percentage of total costs.
- Labour retention and labour turnover.

By analysing the functional areas of the business, managers will gain an insight into the strengths and weaknesses of the organisation and this will influence the strategic planning.

There are various models that managers can use to analyse certain aspects of business performance. These include the Triple Bottom Line, and Kaplan and Nortons' Balanced Scorecard.

Whilst financial measures of performance are commonly used businesses and stakeholders may well use other measures as well. By using a range of measures it may give a better view of the overall performance of the business.

The **Triple Bottom Line** measures the performance of a business in terms of Profit, People and Planet. This means that as well as measuring profits, managers also consider:

- The impact of their actions on the planet i.e. the impact the environment.
- The impact on the people in the business i.e. the impact on employees.

It may be possible, for example, that Business A makes high profits but does so at the expense of the environment and treats its employees badly. Business B might have lower profits but be a very good employer in terms of the conditions and benefits it provides. It may also recycle and reuse much of its materials and take actions to be environmentally friendly. Although B is less profitable it may be seen as having a better overall performance using the Triple Bottom Line.

Another method of assessing performance is known as the Balanced Scorecard. The Balanced Scorecard, developed by Kaplan and Norton, measures performance in relation to:

- Its finances.
- The customer perspective, i.e. what do customers think about the business? What is the degree of customer loyalty?
- An internal business process perspective, i.e. how efficient is the business? Does it have many products in development?
- A learning and growth perspective, i.e. how trained are employees? Do they have the skills they need for the future?

Again, the value of this type of assessment method is that it considers more than just the finances. For example, a business may be highly profitable at the moment but analysis of the customer perspective may show a high level of dissatisfaction and a lack of customer retention. This is useful to know because it may threaten future profits. Similarly, a business may have high profits now but little investment in products for the future suggesting that profits may not be so good in the future.

How to analyse data

Managers will not just analyse the current data; they will want to look at what is happening over time and how data may change in the future. For example, a sudden one-off drop in sales due to bad weather is different from a long-term decline in sales. A jump in costs due to a sudden jump in oil prices is different from a long-term increase in labour costs compared to revenue generated. It is important to analyse the trend to understand the overall picture of where the business is heading. It will also be important to forecast, as what matters is not what has happened but what is going to happen. A business that has

Key term

Triple Bottom Line: measure of the performance of a business in terms of Profit, People and Planet.

Activity

Research a company of your choice. Identify the measures of performance used by the business apart from financial ones. Why do you think the business has chosen these indicators of performance?

Link

Part of assessing the performance of a business may be to examine its impact on stakeholders. To find out more about stakeholders read Chapter 1.

had its highest profits ever has done well but managers would still be worried if a major decline is predicted in all future years.

To understand the context of data, managers will want to compare with other businesses. If your sales are rising by 1% this may be good, but if everyone else's is rising by 10% you are actually losing market share. A decline in profits by 2% may be a worry, but if the economy is in recession and others are losing 30% then, relatively, your performance has been quite good.

It is important therefore when assessing the position of the business for managers to consider:

- What were they expecting given the resources allocated to this area?
- How does it compare with previous years?
- What is it expected to do in the future?
- How does it compare with other businesses?

This analysis should lead to action being taken to improve performance.

Progress questions

15 Explain the difference between the profit margin and the return on capital employed.
16 State two shareholder ratios.
17 State two efficiency ratios.
18 What is a profit centre?
19 State the three elements of performance measured by the Triple Bottom Line.

Exam-style questions

Explanation and analysis

1   Explain one reason why a low current ratio might be of concern to managers.   (4 marks)

2   Explain two ratios a potential supplier of a business might examine before deciding whether to accept the contract.   (6 marks)

3   Explain two ratios a potential investor in a business might examine before deciding whether to invest.   (6 marks)

4   Analyse why a high gearing ratio might be of concern to managers.   (9 marks)

5   Analyse why introducing profit centres may be useful to managers of national chain of shops.   (9 marks)

Evaluation

6   You want to invest in the shares of a business. Do you think you should undertake financial ratio analysis based on its last set of accounts? Assess the arguments for and against and make a judgement.   (12 marks)

7   You are assessing the financial performance of a business. Do you think you should focus more on profitability ratios or liquidity ratios? Assess the arguments for and against and make a judgement.   (12 marks)

3 Analysing the industry environment

The industry environment

The **industry environment** describes the conditions of the industry in which a business is operating. This environment is analysed using a model developed by Michael Porter in 1980 called Five Forces Analysis.

Porter's Five Forces Analysis (see Figure 3.1) involves an examination of the competitive conditions in an industry and the relationship between existing businesses and their buyers and suppliers. By analysing the various forces in an industry this helps us (and managers) to understand why some industries are more profitable than others.

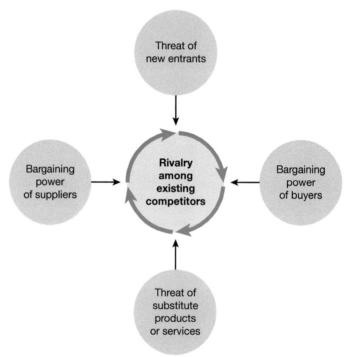

▲ **Figure 3.1**: Porter's Five Forces Analysis

Five Forces Analysis considers the degree of competition in an industry by analysing:

1   **The degree of rivalry.** The more intense the rivalry between businesses the more they are competing with each other. Profits are likely to be lower when there is high rivalry because businesses will use lower price to compete. If there is little rivalry and the businesses work together they could push up prices together and increase profits. The degree of rivalry in an industry will depend on:

- how many businesses there are in an industry; the more businesses there are the greater the rivalry is likely to be
- the relative size of the businesses; if they are similar sizes this increases the degree of rivalry whereas if one was much larger than others it may have the power to force them to work together
- how they compete. If businesses compete mainly on price then this will tend to lead to lower prices as they attempt to out compete each other; this brings down profits. If, however, they compete by differentiating their brands or in after sales service they may be able to maintain relatively high prices and profit margins.

2 **The extent of the entry threat.** This measures how easy it is for other businesses to enter the industry. The easier it is for this to happen the lower the profits of the existing businesses are likely to be. If profits are particularly high, other businesses enter and bring them down by increasing the competition in the market. If, however, the entry threat is low this means that existing businesses can earn high profits without others entering to compete these away. The threat of entry depends on the barriers to entry into an industry.

Barriers to entry include:

- **brand loyalty:** if there is a high degree of brand loyalty customers will be less likely to switch to new entrants, reducing the entry threat.

- **costs of entry:** if entering a market requires heavy investment, e.g. to develop the infrastructure for an energy or telecommunications network, this may make it more difficult to enter.

- **access to resources:** if existing businesses have access to and control of the key supplies or key distribution channels required this is a barrier to entry.

- **government regulation:** some governments use protectionist measures to protect their own businesses from competition. These measures can include taxes on foreign goods, called tariffs, and limits on the quantity of foreign goods allowed in – called quotas). Tariffs increase the price of foreign products and so customers are likely to switch to cheaper domestic products; the tax raised is revenue for the government. Quotas restrict the number of foreign products, so if customers want more than this they have to buy domestic products. Tariffs and quotas make it more difficult for foreign businesses to compete, and they act as a barrier to entry.

> **Key term**
>
> **Barriers to entry:** these make it difficult or expensive for new businesses to enter a market. They include patents, customer/brand loyalty, high start-up costs and limited access to distribution channels.

> **Progress question**
>
> 1 How might increased barriers to entry affect the profits in an industry?

3 **The extent of a substitute threat.** A substitute is a product that is different in form from the one provided by existing businesses but it performs a similar function. For example, an aluminium can or a glass bottle are different products but both sites hold liquids. If there

are many substitutes for a given product this means there are many alternatives. This will reduce the likely profits made because if prices are high customers will switch to the alternatives. A high substitute threat pushes down prices and reduces profits of existing businesses.

Five Forces Analysis, therefore considers the degree of competition that is occurring via rivals, substitutes and the threat of entry. It also considers which businesses in the whole supply chain have the power.

4 **The degree of buyer power:** if the buyers of the products are very powerful they will push down prices and reduce the profits of the producers. The buyer may be the end customer or the distributor or the retailer. The stronger these buyers are the more they can bargain and reduce the price and profits of the business producing for them. Buyer power will be higher if:

   – there are relatively few buyers so the producers have little choice but to accept what they are offered

   – the buyer has the choice of many different products to choose from and can therefore bargain strongly.

5 **Supplier power.** Businesses will be buying inputs in from their suppliers. If the suppliers are powerful they can push up prices; this increases their profits but reduces the profits of their customers. Suppliers will be powerful if there are few of them so the businesses they sell to have little bargaining power. For example, there are relatively few producers of aircraft engines in the world; this means they have a lot of power when negotiating with aircraft manufacturers who need their product.

▼ **Table 3.1**: Summary of the five forces

Force	Scale	Effect on profits of established businesses
Buyer power	high	Pushes down prices and reduces profits.
Supplier power	high	Suppliers push up their prices increasing businesses costs and reducing their profits.
Rivalry	high	Increased competition reducing prices and profits.
Entry threat	high	Puts pressure on established businesses to keep profits low or entry will occur.
Substitute threat	high	Gives buyers more choice and therefore keeps prices and profits lower.

Changing the five forces

The existing businesses do not have to accept the five forces. They can try to change them and make them more favourable.

For example:

- Rivalry can be reduced by taking over rivals or merging with them. Alternatively, businesses can try to remove the competition, perhaps through price cutting.
- Supplier power can be reduced by producing inputs itself or taking over a supplier to gain control of it.
- Buyer power can be reduced by developing a strong brand.
- Substitute threat can be reduced by taking over substitutes or promoting the unique features of what they offer.

Activity

Research an industry of your choice. Decide on the strength of each of the five forces in this industry. Justify your decisions.

Get it right

Remember that the forces may not all have the same effects on profits. There may be an industry with high buyer power but low entry threat for example or one with high rivalry but low supplier power. What matters is the overall effect the combined forces have.

Progress questions

4   How might a manager try to increase the barriers to entry into an industry?

5   How might a manager try to reduce rivalry in an industry?

6   How might greater buyer power in an industry affect profits?

Case study

Ofo

Ofo is a bike rental business that was set up in China just a few years ago. For a short time this was an extraordinarily successful business and you can find its bikes all over China. Customers paid a deposit and could then use a bike by scanning a QR code. Once they had got to their destination they left the bike there for someone else to use. However, customers began to worry about the financial position of the business and started to demand their deposits back. Concern over the ability of the company to pay led to even more people asking for their money back. At one point the company had a valuation of $2 billion, but the value fell dramatically once confidence in its finances collapsed.

Part of Ofo's problems was that it expanded too fast. Another problem was the fierce competition from other providers. It also faced challenges in the form of rising costs to repair the bikes that were vandalised or broken. Fighting for market share was expensive for Ofo (and its rivals) and it struggled to generate profits.

At its peak, Ofo had bikes in more than 20 countries, from France to Australia and the United States. But more recently it has had to pull out of many of these markets.

1   With reference to Porter's five forces, analyse the reasons why bike rental companies such as Ofo are struggling to make a profit.

2   To what extent do you think it is inevitable that bike rentals will stop being offered in future?

Case study

Sonos

The Sonos speaker company was established in 2002 near Silicon Valley. Its speakers are now owned by over seven million households. They are so popular that customers are often existing owners. More than 2/5 of buyers already have a Sonos speaker. These speakers are popular because they can link easily with online music and news providers and the software automatically updates.

For several years Sonos had little competition but recently it has been challenged by the growth of "smart speakers". Smart speakers are wireless audio devices that obey voice command, such as Alexa. Nearly 100 million smart speakers have been sold, mainly by Amazon and Google. They generally do not match Sonos on sound quality but appeal in terms of price and service.

Sonos could react by selling cheaper speakers but it would need to be careful of starting a price war with Amazon and Google. Instead, Sonos has decided to focus on differentiating itself. It has developed new forms of its speakers, such as sound bars for televisions, and is working with Ikea on integrating speakers into the furniture company's products.

However, investors remain uncertain whether this strategy will work and Sonos' shares have fallen in price since it

became a public limited company. Investors are worried about the competition from companies such as Amazon.

Sonos does have one big advantage over some of its rivals. As a pioneer of wireless speakers, it has always led In terms of speaker technology. It has around 700 patents, including ones for how music can be streamed to speakers and how these can be tuned to the acoustics of the room they are in. It has reportedly allowed Google to use its intellectual property in return for making Assistant available on its devices.

1   Analyse the strength of two of Porter's five forces in this industry.

2   Do you think Sonos should cut its prices? Assess the case for and against and make a judgement.

Progress questions

7   Explain what is meant by entry threat.

8   Explain the difference between rivalry and the substitute threat.

9   What is meant by buyer power?

10 What is meant by supplier power?

11 Explain one way a business can change one of the five forces.

Exam-style questions

Explanation and analysis

1 Explain one way an increase in buyer power might affect the profits of an industry. (4 marks)

2 Explain one way a business might reduce the power of suppliers in its industry. (4 marks)

3 Explain two ways a business might reduce the threat of entry into the industry. (6 marks)

4 Analyse how a greater substitute threat might affect the profits in an industry. (9 marks)

5 Analyse how less rivalry might affect the profits in an industry. (9 marks)

Evaluation

6 You are the Chief Executive of a business. Do you think you have to accept the impact of the five forces in an industry on your profits? Assess the arguments for and against and make a judgement. (12 marks)

7 Do you think the internet has made the five forces more or less favourable for most industries? Assess the arguments for and against and make a judgement. (12 marks)

4 Analysing the external environment to assess opportunities and threats: political and legal change

This section will develop your knowledge and understanding of:

→ The impact of changes in the political and legal environment on strategy and the functional areas.

Business strategy is influenced by the external environment. This includes the political and legal environment. Changes in the political or legal situation create opportunities and threats for businesses. The political and legal environments differ enormously between countries. Managers working in different countries must recognise these differences and adapt accordingly.

The legal environment

The legal environment refers to laws passed by the government. These include:

- **Competition laws.** These may exist to protect some businesses from the actions of others. For example, large businesses may dominate an industry and use their power to force smaller businesses to close. Large businesses may undercut smaller ones or may pressurise distributors not to deal with them making it difficult for them to sell their products. Laws to make sure big firms do not abuse their power are often called anti-trust or anti-monopoly laws. These laws are also intended to protect consumers from being forced to pay higher prices or accept poor quality because a dominant business knows they have little choice. For example, competition law may regulate businesses wanting to merge or take over another; governments will want to ensure that if the integration did go ahead the bigger business would not abuse its power.

- **Consumer laws.** These are intended to protect consumers. They may include laws:
  - to ensure products have certain details on their labels
  - affecting the safety of products
  - affecting the way that products are advertised and described
  - affecting what can be sold and when and where it can be sold.

  For example, in many countries laws have been passed to control the marketing and sales of cigarettes because of the damage this product can causes to peoples' health. In some countries there are strict regulations on what is on the packaging on cigarettes to ensure the health dangers are clear as well as controls on the way they are advertised and controls on who is targeted in the advertisements to protect children. In many countries recently there have been laws introduced to limit the amount of sugar in children's foods to protect their health.

- **Employment laws.** In many countries, laws will exist to protect employees. These may include:
  - safety laws which ensure that working conditions are safe
  - minimum wage laws to ensure employees receive a certain amount of money for the work done

Link

The effect of changes in the external environment on the strategy selected can be shown using SWOT analysis. You can find out more about SWOT analysis in Chapter 1.

- discrimination laws to protect certain groups at work
- redundancy laws to give employees some protection if the business is going to close
- other employment rights such as the right to have a contract, the right to sick pay or the right for time off work when a child is born.

- **Laws on trade.** Laws on trade and international trading agreements may affect what trade can be undertaken between countries. A government may limit the import or export of certain products from other countries for political or economic reasons. This can affect costs and availability of materials and the ease of access to overseas markets.

- **Environmental laws.** Many governments have passed laws in recent years to protect the environment. These laws might include:
  - controlling emissions
  - limiting pollution
  - encouraging sustainable energy
  - reducing the consumption of plastic
  - encouraging the switching to electric vehicles.

  These environmental laws will create new markets for some (e.g. electric cars) whilst damaging the markets for others (e.g. diesel cars). They can increase costs because of restrictions on how production is carried out; they can also reduce costs, for example by reducing waste and encouraging recycling.

- **Laws on taxes and subsidies.** Laws passed linked to government spending and taxation will affect businesses costs and demand. For example, a government may want to encourage start-ups by providing subsidies (finance) to help new businesses or by reducing some of the taxes they have to pay. Equally a government may want to discourage tobacco consumptions and so pass laws to tax this product heavily.

The effect of changes in the legal environment

Laws can:

- Increase costs: for example, by increasing the requirements for safe working conditions and giving employees more rights (such as the right to pay if they are sick).
- Restrict the ability to sell in certain markets: for example, due to trade disagreements a business may not be allowed to export to some countries.
- Restrict the ability of businesses to make decisions: for example, an effort to take over another business may be prevented.

However, laws may also have positive effects for some businesses.

- They may protect them from anti-competitive behaviour by other businesses (such as false advertising or bullying suppliers).
- They mean there are certain standards that all businesses have to meet which prevent some from providing cheaper but unsafe products.
- They may open up markets; for example; a new trade deal may make trade possible with a new country.

Activity

Research a recent change in the law in your country. Research why it was introduced and how it has affected business.

Case study

Johnson & Johnson

The price of shares in the US company Johnson & Johnson
fell significantly in 2018 after a report that it had known
about there being traces of asbestos in its talcum powder
for decades. The report came as the company faced many
lawsuits claiming that its talcum products caused cancer.
A review of Johnson and Johnson's actions suggest some
staff knew about the asbestos since 1971. The company's
lawyers claim that its talcum powder is safe.

In July 2018 Johnson and Johnson had to pay $4.47 billion
(£3.6 billion) in damages to 22 women who alleged that its
talculm powder had led them to develop ovarian cancer. The
company is appealing against this decision.

1 Explain one reason why laws are necessary to
   protect consumers.

2 To what extent do you think laws make it more difficult
   for businesses to make profit? Assess the case for and
   against and make a judgement.

The political environment

The nature and role of government will vary from one country to
another. For example, in some countries there are elections every
five years, in others one party governs without regular elections. In
some countries the government is very interventionist; this means
that the government intervenes in the economy, society and business
a great deal. For example, the government might provide most of
the goods and services in an economy such as energy, transport,
telecommunications, education and health. These are sometimes called
"planned' or "command" economies because much of what happens
is planned or commanded by the government. Other countries are
more free market. This means that they leave the provision of more
goods and services to business. People are allowed to set up in business
and provide a range of products. Of course, even in free markets the
government will intervene in some areas to protect citizens and ensure
they have essential services.

Countries such as China, Cuba and North Korea have been
interventionist, although in recent years have allowed more businesses
to operate for themselves. Countries such as the USA and the UK are
more free market with less government intervention.

The more interventionist a government is:

*   The more products will be provided by the government rather than
    private businesses. This may restrict the range of products available
    because individual businesses are not trying to develop their own
    goods and services.
*   The more employees will work for the government.

Government intervention in a country can be very beneficial because:

*   Governments will plan for the welfare of society. There may be
    some services or products that are not very profitable but are good
    for society – for example some transport may be essential to help
    people get around the country even if some routes may not be very

profitable. The government may also ensure that the prices of some products are not too high; they can keep the price of energy low, for example, to ensure everyone can heat their homes.

- Governments may plan for the long term. Private businesses often have to make quite quick returns for their owners. People invest in a business and want to see profits within a few years. A government may be more willing to invest in projects such as major construction projects that may take many years to earn a return.

- Governments can regulate what is provided. This can control the provision of undesirable products, such as drugs, whilst encouraging the production of other products which may be regarded as desirable even if they are not very profitable, such as green space or play areas.

However, government intervention may:

- Remove the incentive to innovate. If the government controls what is produced then there may be little incentive to develop new products and processes. In the free market entrepreneurs can earn the rewards from innovations. This may mean there are more new products and greater variety of products in a free market compared to a planned economy.

- Lead to bad business decisions. Politicians may not be particularly good at making the right business decision; this can lead to over- or under-production or poor quality.

The effect of political stability or instability

One political factor businesses will consider is the degree of political stability in a county. This will affect how attractive a country is to business. If there is a high level of instability, for example, if it is likely the existing government will be overthrown or, in an extreme case, the country is in a state of civil war, managers may be wary of investing because the future is so uncertain. If a country has a stable government, for example, if there is no question of it being replaced in the near future and it is very popular with its citizens, this may make it more likely that a manager will invest because there is greater certainty about the state of the country in the coming years.

The effect of corruption within an economy

Corruption occurs when people with authority misuse their power. They act fraudulently. Corruption usually involves bribes. For example, a business may pay money to the personal bank account of a government minister in order to:

- Win a contract a business might pay money to a government minister.

- Gain the exclusive rights to provide a product.

Corruption in some countries is almost part of daily life; to get something done you have to use your influence (e.g. the power of someone you know) or pay money illegally to get something done.

> **Key term**
>
> **Corruption:** occurs when people with authority misuse their power.

Corruption:

- Can increase costs because in order to do business a manager has to pay extra money.
- Can lead to poor-quality and even dangerous products because contracts can go to the business that pays the most illegally rather than the best provider.
- Can put off businesses that want to behave legally because they will not win contracts unless they cheat as well. This can reduce competition and reduce the quality of services provided.

The Corruption Perceptions Index is a measure of corruption within countries.

Each year Transparency International scores countries on how corrupt their government sectors are seen to be.

▼ Table 4.1: Extract from the 2018 Corruption Perceptions Index showing the least corrupt countries in 2018

#	COUNTRY	REGION	2018
1	Denmark	Western Europe & European Union	88
2	New Zealand	Asia Pacific	87
3	Finland	Western Europe & European Union	85
3	Singapore	Asia Pacific	85
3	Sweden	Western Europe & European Union	85

To reduce corruption, Transparency International argues that there needs to be:

- Free speech.
- An independent media.
- Minimised regulations on media, including traditional laws that focus on access to information and that are implemented. This access would help to enhance transparency and accountability while reducing opportunities for corruption.

By encouraging openness in the media this should highlight corruption and make people less willing to take bribes for fear that it will be revealed by the media.

Progress questions

1. Explain one way an employment law might affect a business.
2. Explain one way competition law might affect a business.
3. Explain one way an environmental law might affect a business.
4. State one way in which political instability might affect a business.
5. State one way in which corruption can affect a business.

Exam-style questions

Explanation and analysis

1 Explain one way laws can affect the profits of a business. (4 marks)

2 Explain one way that political instability might affect business investment. (4 marks)

3 Explain two ways that giving employees more rights might affect a business. (6 marks)

4 Analyse how corruption in an economy might affect business in that country. (9 marks)

5 Analyse why the government might want to help entrepreneurs to start up in business. (9 marks)

Evaluation

6 You have been asked to pay a bribe to win a major contract that would lead to high profits and save jobs. Should you pay the bribe? Assess the arguments for and against and make a judgement. (12 marks)

7 You are the Chief Executive of a large hotel business. Do you think changes in the law will always reduce your profits? Assess the arguments for and against and make a judgement. (12 marks)

5 Analysing the external environment to assess opportunities and threats: economic change

This section will develop your knowledge and understanding of:

→ The impact of changes in the national and global economic environment on strategy and the functional areas.

→ The importance of globalisation for business.

When managers are planning what to do next they must take into account the economic environment that their business operates in.

Changes in economic factors can affect demand and costs and therefore profits.

The main economic factors affecting a business are:

- **Gross Domestic Product (GDP):** this measures the national income of a country.
- **Taxation rates:** these are charges that may be paid to the government by customers, households, employees and businesses.
- **The exchange rate:** this measures the price of one currency in terms of another; for example, the price of dollars in terms of yen.
- **Inflation:** this measures how much prices in general are increasing over a given period.
- **Deflation:** this measures how much prices in general are decreasing over a given period. This is less common than inflation.
- **Unemployment:** this measures the number of people who want to work but who do not have a job.
- **Interest rates:** this measures the cost of borrowing money and the rate of return paid to people who save money by the banks.
- **Trade:** this refers to the buying and selling of goods and services between countries.
- **Infrastructure:** refers to the communications, energy and transport systems that exist within a country.
- **Resources:** these are inputs such as labour, land and capital; changes in the availability and prices of these resources can be important to businesses.

Managers will want to try to anticipate any changes in these factors. They may do this by monitoring the news and government forecasts and/or commission their own research and consultants.

Gross Domestic Product

The Gross Domestic Product (GDP) of a particular country measures the total income earned by households and businesses in a country over a given time period, usually a year. For example, GDP would include the profits, wages, and rent earned in a country. GDP is also called national income. Changes in national income are important because they can affect the demand for various goods and services. In general more income should lead to more demand, but the impact will depend on what types of products are being considered.

Activity

Find one story in the news that you think is related to the economic environment. Briefly explain how the factor in the economic environment that you have identified has affected business.

Activity

Look at the news in your country Can you identify the following in your country at the moment?
- The growth in national income.
- The inflation rate.
- The unemployment rate.
- The interest rate.

Link

Changes in the economic environment will create Opportunities and Threats. This can affect the strategy selected using SWOT analysis. For more information on SWOT analysis see Chapter 1.

▼ Table 5.1: Overview of income elasticity of demand

Factor	Meaning
Positive answer	Means that when income increases, quantity demanded increases. This is a normal product.
Negative answer	Means that when income increases, quantity demanded decreases and vice versa. This is an inferior product.
Value of more than 1	Income elastic; the percentage change in quantity demanded is greater than the percentage change in income. This is a luxury product.
Value of less than 1	Income inelastic; the percentage change in quantity demanded is less than the percentage change in income. This is a necessity product.

For luxury (income elastic) goods, consumer demand is more responsive to a change in income, so when income increases so demand for income elastic goods increases by more than the increase in income (in percentage terms). For example, diamonds are a luxury good that are income elastic. Income elastic means a given percentage change in income leads to a greater percentage change in demand.

For income inelastic goods, consumer demand rises less proportionately in response to an increase in income. Examples include gas, electricity, water, drinks, clothing and food. Income inelastic means a given percentage change in income leads to a smaller percentage change in demand.

For inferior goods (for example, value brand coffee), the demand will actually fall when income increases: demand of inferior goods is inversely related to the income of a consumer. For example, people may switch from bicycles as their chosen form of transport to cars as their income increases. Or they might swap from value brand coffee to top-of-the range barista coffee.

Managers will monitor income in their own country (as this will affect domestic demand) and abroad as this will affect demand from other countries. Businesses are increasingly global and often sell in several markets overseas. Income levels abroad can therefore be important to total sales and to decisions in the different functional areas.

▼ Table 5.2: GDP and the functional areas

Functional areas	Possible impact of an increase in GDP (national income)
Marketing	May consider increasing prices if people can pay more, may introduce more premium range items.
Operations	May increase output if sales rise.
Human Resources	May need to recruit more staff, may find it more difficult to recruit if unemployment is low as businesses generally recruiting.
Finance	Profits may rise with higher sales.

Case study

GDP

1 State how much has the world's national income typically increased each year.
2 Analyse how these changes in world GDP might affect demand for goods and services.
3 To what extent do you think GDP determines the success of a business? Assess the case for and against, and make a judgement.

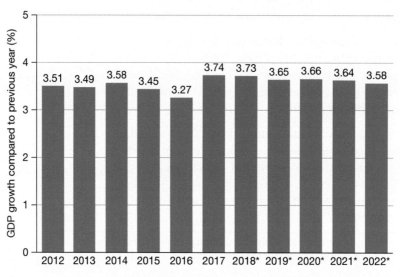

▲ Figure 5.1: Growth of the global gross domestic product (GDP) from 2012 to 2022 (compared to the previous year)

Taxation

Taxes are charges that a government uses to raise revenue and also to discourage consumption (for example, governments may tax cigarettes to reduce the amount smoked).

Taxes may be:

- Charged on the amount people earn or businesses make in profits. These are called direct taxes because they are charged directly on the money earned.
- Charged on the products when they are sold; these are called indirect taxes because consumers pay them when they buy the product and the businesses pay them to the government.

Taxes may affect:

- Demand: for example, tax on diesel cars may encourage customers to switch to electric vehicles.
- Costs: for example, higher taxes on imported products can increase costs and if these cannot be passed on to consumers they will reduce profits.
- Investment: higher taxes now or in the future may affect the expected profits of any project and therefore affect investment levels.

▼ Table 5.3: Changes in taxation and the functional areas

Functional areas	Possible impact of an increase in income tax
Marketing	Demand may be lower with lower incomes after tax; marketing may consider how to maintain or boost sales in this situation, e.g special offers, lower price range items; may seek market overseas.
Operations	May reduce output if sales rise.
Human Resources	May need to recruit less staff or even make redundancies; may face demands for higher wages because of higher taxes.
Finance	Profits may fall with lower sales.

Exchange rates

An exchange rate is the price of one currency in terms of another.

If the exchange rate of one currency against another increases in value this means it has got "stronger" or "appreciated" in value. For example, if 1 Egyptian pound was 0.05 US dollars and then became worth 0.1 US dollars then the Egyptian pound has become stronger. It costs more in dollars.

The effect of a strong currency is that it will cost buyers abroad more in their currency to buy the products. The domestic price remains the same but more foreign currency is needed to get pay the domestic price.

▼ Table 5.4: Example of impact of stronger currency on export prices

Price in Egypt	Egyptian pound exchange rate	Price of product in US dollars
100 EGP	1 EGP = 0.05 US dollars	100 × 0.05 = $5
100 EGP	1 EGP = 0.1 US dollars	100 × 0.1 = $10

A strong currency is likely to lead to a fall in sales abroad. The extent to which sales fall depend on how price sensitive demand is.

To try and avoid a fall in sales a business might:

- Promote its products more, stressing why they are value for money even at a higher price.
- Keep the price the same abroad and in return receive less domestic currency and make less profit per item.

If the exchange rate of one currency falls in value against another it is "weaker" and has "depreciated". This means that an item would sell for less in terms of the foreign currency. Other things unchanged, this should lead to an increase in sales. If managers expect this to occur they will want to consider if they have enough production capacity.

▼ Table 5.5: Example of impact of weaker currency of export prices

Price of product in Thai baht	Thai baht against dollar exchange rate	Price of product in US dollars
100	1 baht = 0.03 dollars	100 × 0.03 = $3
100	1 baht = 0.01 dollars	100 × 0.01 = $1

Changes in the exchange rate also affect the costs of a business. This is because many materials are bought in from abroad.

A stronger currency means it has more purchasing power abroad and can buy more of the foreign currency. This means less of your own currency needs to be spent to buy the same things as before. This reduces costs.

▼ Table 5.6: Example of impact of a stronger currency on import costs

Price of US products	Egyptian pound exchange rate	Price of product in US dollars
$10	1 EGP = 0.05 US dollars	10 × 0.05 = $10/0.05 = 200 EGP
$10	1 EGP = 0.1 US dollars	10 × 0.1 = 10 EGP

A weaker currency means it has less purchasing power abroad and can buy less of the foreign currency. This means more of your own currency needs to be spent to buy the same things as before. This increases costs.

▼ Table 5.7: Summary of exchange rate changes

Change in one currency in terms of another	Effect on price of exports abroad	Likely effect on sales abroad	Effect on price of imports in own currency	Impact on costs of imported materials
More expensive	Increase	Less	Less	Less
Cheaper	Decrease	Increase	More	More

The impact of any change in currency will depend on:

- How much it changes (and some currencies change value frequently and significantly).
- Which currencies it changes against. The US dollar, for example, might become more expensive in relation to the Japanese Yen but weaker against the European euro. It is important to know which currency movement is being analysed.

Exchange rate volatility

The value of an exchange rate will depend on the demand for that currency and the supply i.e. how much people and businesses want to change into another currency. If demand is high this is likely to pull up the value of the currency and the exchange rate rises; if the supply is high this will reduce the value of a currency. Supply and demand conditions for any currency change all the time and this means that an exchange rate can vary significantly in short periods of time. This means exchange rates can be volatile. This volatility can make it difficult to plan because of the uncertainty of costs or the price

Activities

Research what has happened to the value of your currency in recent years.

1   Why do you think these changes may have happened?

2   How do you think these changes may have affected businesses in your country?

of a good in foreign currency. Exchange rate volatility can reduce investment because of the uncertainty and may mean a business avoids trading in that region.

Case study

Malaysian Ringitt

The chart below shows the value of the US dollar in terms of Malaysian Ringitt over time.

▲ Figure 5.2: US Dollar to Malaysian Ringgit Chart

1   What was the approximate value of a US dollar in terms of Malaysian Ringitts:

   a   at the start of 2009   **b**   the start of 2017

2   Analyse the likely effects of these changes between 2009 and 2017 on businesses in Malaysia.

▼ Table 5.8: Exchange rate changes and functional areas

Functional areas	Possible impact of an increase in exchange rate
Marketing	May reduce sales as price is more expensive in foreign currency, marketing may try to promote the benefits offered to justify this price and/or may target other markets if this is going to be a long-term issue.
	May face more competition domestically from lower price foreign competition (as strong currency means imports are cheaper).
Operations	May seek to reduce costs to enable a lower price overseas but profit margins to be maintained.
	May switch to more overseas suppliers as currency has more purchasing lower and imports cheaper.
Human Resources	May have to make redundancies if the higher price overseas affects sales significantly.
Finance	Profits may fall with lower sales overseas but this may be offset by cheaper imported supplies, depends on how dependent overseas sales and imports to the business is.

Inflation

Inflation occurs when prices generally are increasing over a given period. For example if inflation is 2% this means that prices are generally going to be 2% higher by the end of the year than at the start.

Inflation may occur because:

- Demand is high in the economy and businesses feel able to push up their prices.
- Costs are high (perhaps because of higher wages or higher import costs) and businesses decide to push up prices to protect their profit margins.

Inflation may be important because:

- It may mean higher costs for inputs. Managers need to decide whether they can pass on any increase to customers. If managers feel demand for their products is too sensitive to risk increasing price they may have to accept higher costs and lower profit margins.
- It may mean employees demand higher wages to compensate for higher prices, This can further increase costs.
- If inflation rates are difficult to predict and plan for this may affect investment levels by the business. If managers are uncertain about what costs and selling prices are going to be this may reduce the amount of projects they want to go ahead with.

▼ Table 5.9: The impact of inflation on functional areas

Functional areas	Possible impact of inflation on functional areas
Marketing	May consider increasing prices to cover higher costs; will depend on how sensitive price is for this product.
Operations	May seek to reduce costs to offset higher input costs.
Human Resources	May face demands for higher wages because of higher prices.
Finance	Profits may fall with higher costs; may deter investment if there is uncertainty about future price movements.

Key term

Inflation: is a sustained increase in the general price level over a given period of time.

Activity

Research the rate of inflation in your economy. How does this inflation affect businesses in your country?

Deflation

Deflation occurs when the general price level of products in general is falling over a given period of time. This can lead to consumers and business delaying spending because they wait for lower prices later on. This delay in spending means less demand which in itself can lead to lower prices. This can lead to a spiral downwards of low demand and falling prices.

Free trade

If there are no barriers to trade this means businesses can:

- Access resources from all over the world. This means they can find the cheapest, best quality supplies.
- Sell to customers all over the world; this increases the potential sales of the business.

Free trade occurs when goods and services flow freely between
countries without any barriers. Free trade allows businesses to find
the best value suppliers anywhere in the world and sell wherever they
wish. However, it does also open businesses up to competition from all
over the world. This can be bad for particular businesses that are not
very competitive because they will face global competition. In some
countries a whole industry may not be very competitive and free trade
could prove a high risk for them.

▼ Table 5.10: Free trade and functional areas

Functional areas	Possible impact of free trade on functional areas
Marketing	May target new overseas countries as there is easier access; may face greater competition domestically.
Operations	May increase output if sales rise; may consider producing overseas if there is now easier access; may use more international suppliers.
Human Resources	May need to recruit more staff; may recruit from overseas as the business may have access to more talent globally.
Finance	Profits may rise with higher sales overseas and access to lower costs supplies; however, may suffer due to greater foreign competition domestically.

To protect local businesses governments may introduce barriers to
trade (known as protectionism) such as tariffs, quotas or regulatory
requirements that foreign businesses have to meet.

Examples of **protectionism** include:

- A tariff is a tax on imported foreign goods and services which
  makes them relatively expensive.
- A quota is a limit on the number of foreign goods and services
  which restricts their sales.
- Regulatory requirements can introduce standards and criteria that
  foreign products must meet which make it difficult for them to
  compete or be allowed into a country.

Protectionism:

- Protects a domestic industry. This means local businesses with
  higher costs and possibly less good-quality products than their
  foreign rivals can survive.
- Makes it difficult for foreign businesses to compete.

However, whilst protectionism may seem appealing in fact it:

- Can lead to retaliation from the other country; this can reduce the
  opportunities to sell abroad.
- May encourage businesses to be complacent and allows them
  to survive even if they are inefficient. This can cause problems
  when there is more competition with business globally (e.g. when
  protectionist measures are removed) as these businesses will
  struggle to compete).
- Increases prices and reduces choice for consumers which may
  prove unpopular over time.

Key terms

Protectionism: occurs when a
country introduces measures to
protect its own producers against
foreign competition.

Free trade: occurs when there is no
protectionism.

▼ Table 5.11: The effect of protectionism on functional areas

Functional areas	Possible impact of greater protectionism on functional areas
Marketing	May be able to increase prices in a protected market; may not need to promote as aggressively if there is less competition.
Operations	May increase output if sales rise due to lack of foreign competition; however, may lose sales overseas if there is retaliation.
Human Resources	May need to recruit more staff of demand is higher domestically.
Finance	Profits may rise with higher sales domestically.

Progress question

4   A government has previously introduced protectionist measures to protect local businesses. How do you think the removal of these measures might affect local businesses?

Interest rates

Interest rates are the reward that you get for saving money in a bank and the cost of borrowing money. If the interest rate for saving was 2% per year this would mean that if you saved $100 you would receive $102 back at the end of the year. If the rate for borrowing was 2% per year then if you borrowed $100 you would have to repay $102 a year later.

If interest rates are high this means:

*   It is expensive to borrow. This means businesses are less likely to borrow money for investment. It also means consumers are less likely to borrow to buy products. Higher interest rates can, therefore, reduce demand and increase costs; both of which squeeze profits.
*   Higher interest rates can be attractive to people and businesses abroad that want to gain higher returns by saving in a country. This can lead to an increase in demand for that currency from abroad increasing the exchange rate. A higher exchange rate can make exports abroad more expensive in foreign currency and imports cheaper in pounds. This can make domestic businesses uncompetitive because their products will be more expensive in terms of foreign currency and foreign products will be cheaper in the domestic currency.

The impact of an interest rate change will be greater if:

*   A business is highly geared (i.e has a high proportion of borrowed funds).
*   The interest rate change is significant.
*   Demand for the business's products is sensitive to interest rates.

Activity

Research the rate of interest in your economy. What effect does this inflation have on businesses in your country?

Progress question

5   How do you think an increase in interest rates might affect a housebuilding business?

Infrastructure

The infrastructure refers to the basic structures and facilities of a country such as buildings, roads, rail links, airports and power supplies.

The quality and extent of investment in the infrastructure of a country will either make it easier or more difficult to undertake business. It will affect how easy it is to set up a business and how easy it is to run it efficiently. For example, if there is an excellent coverage of superfast broadband this will make it easier for people to set up an online business anywhere in the country. If on the other hand, the internet is slow in some regions this will make it more difficult to run an ecommerce business. If the transport system is good then getting supplies regularly and on time will be easy; if the transport system is unreliable then the business may suffer from running out of supplies or might find it expensive and complex to distribute to its customers.

Prices of resources

Businesses will need resources. The precise mix of resources will depend on the business. Farmers need a relatively high proportion of land. Manufacturing companies need a relatively high level of equipment. Hairdressers and schools are very reliant on people. The prices of these different resources will affect the costs and the profits of the business.

The prices of resources are likely to be influenced by:

- The demand for them; if there is an increase in demand for computer programmers this will probably increase their wages.
- Supply in their markets; if land is in short supply in a city this is likely to make it more expensive.
- Government taxes; this can increase the price of a product.

Some resource prices, such as energy and commodities (e.g. wheat and coffee beans) can be quite volatile due to sudden changes in supply. Major changes in prices can have a big impact on the profitability of the business. Imagine that conflict in a region reduces the amount of oil in the world; this will increase its price and increase costs. The higher costs will reduce the profits of many businesses that depend on oil for their energy and transport.

Two markets that are often especially important for business are:

- **Oil.** Oil is major source of energy for businesses and for their transport. If oil prices increase this increases the costs of business and if businesses cannot pass these costs on it will reduce profits. The price of oil is determined by global market forces of supply and demand. The supply is determined by the amount of oil that has been found and how much it is worth given the costs of extracting it. The supply of oil is sometimes disrupted by political disputes, or even wars, which can limit the output of some oil-producing countries. A reduction in output can lead to a shortage and an increase in price. The demand for oil depends on the demand for energy and the availability of alternative sources of energy. If the growth of the world economy slows down and there is less oil being produced, demand for oil is likely to reduce and the price will fall. If businesses switch to more environmentally friendly sources of energy such as solar power the price of oil again will fall.

Link

The effect of a change in interest rates depends on how highly geared a business is. To find out more about gearing read Chapter 2.

• **Labour.** The price of labour (called wages or salaries) is influenced by the demand and supply of labour. The demand for labour depends on demand for the product being produced. An increase in demand for computer games increases demand for games developers, which is likely to pull up wage levels. The supply of labour will depend on the number of people in the working population, the skills and experience needed and how appealing the job is. The supply of labour for lawyers, for example, is quite limited because it is so skilled and it takes so long to train. A limited supply means people are scarce and this is likely to lead to high wages. The supply of cleaners is bigger because this is a less skilled job; a higher supply leads to lower wages.

Progress questions

6 What might determine the price of land?

7 Why might the price of oil fall?

8 How might a chain of coffee shops respond to an increase in the price of coffee beans?

Case study

Cobalt mining

In recent years there has been increasing interest in mining cobalt.

This is because it is a key component in the lithium-ion batteries that power electronic devices and electric cars. In the past, cobalt supply depended on the markets for copper and nickel, more valuable metals that are typically extracted alongside cobalt. However, with demand rising and pulling up prices its status as a "by product' is changing.

Mining giants are increasing production in the Democratic Republic of Congo (DRC), where most of the world's cobalt is found. In the US, limited cobalt processing started in 2014 for the first time in about four decades.

Cobalt consumption is now over 122,000 tonnes in 2018, up from about 75,000 tonnes in 2011.

After ore containing cobalt is mined using explosives, it is taken to be refined and turned into metal, blends or

chemical concentrates for use in products such as jet engines, drones and batteries. More than 60% of the world's cobalt is mined in the DRC, while China is the world's leading producer of refined cobalt.

1 Analyse the factors that would influence the price of cobalt.

Progress questions

9 What is the difference between inflation and deflation?

10 What is meant by GDP?

11 Explain one way lower interest rates might affect a business.

12 State two factors that affect the price of oil.

13 State two elements of the infrastructure of an economy.

The importance of globalisation for business

Globalisation in a business context refers to the fact businesses are increasingly operating in a global context and have production facilities or processes in different countries. They buy from abroad and they sell abroad. They do not just operate in their domestic market.

Globalisation has occurred because:

- Improvements in transport make it cheaper and quicker for businesses to transport goods around the world.
- Better and cheaper communications make it possible to run and manage your business in different countries. Better communications also mean customers are more familiar with and open to overseas products.
- Less protectionist measures mean more free trade allowing the movement of goods and services more freely between countries.

Globalisation enables businesses to sell their products in many different countries creating major sales opportunities. It also means they can source resources from more places and make best use of all the skills and resources around the world.

Globalisation means:

- There are social effects. People can move more easily around the world to find work, Managers have access to labour in other countries; they may benefit from cheap labour in some countries where the cost of living is lower and/or skilled labour in some regions where the training and education system may be good. Globalisation also opens the world to worldwide brands; travel almost anywhere in the world and you will find a Starbucks, Coca-Cola and Nike.
- There are economic effects on a country. It may benefit businesses by giving them access to markets overseas and to better or cheaper resources. However, some businesses may suffer as they are now facing greater competition from overseas competitors; this can damage the economy.
- There are technological gains. With more open economies there is a need to be innovative and competitive. This will encourage managers to innovate and develop technology. With more trade ideas will be shared and copied more easily meaning that technological advances in one country will soon appear around the world.
- More trade. Greater globalisation means more open markets, which should encourage more trade around the world.

Exam-style questions

Explanation and analysis

1 Explain one way a good-quality infrastructure might help the profits of a business. (4 marks)

2 Explain one way greater globalisation might affect a business. (4 marks)

3 Explain two ways an increase in the value of a country's currency might affect the profits of an exporter. (6 marks)

4 Analyse how an increase in unemployment in a country might affect a business. (9 marks)

5 Analyse how more free trade might affect the profits of a business. (9 marks)

Evaluation

6 You are a producer of locally made shoes. Should you try and get the government to protect your industry against foreign competition? Assess the arguments for and against and make a judgement.

7 You are expecting the exchange rate of your country's currency to increase against its major trading partner. Should you warn your shareholders that your profits are likely to rise or fall? Assess the arguments for and against and make a judgement.

6 Social, technological and environmental change

This chapter will develop your knowledge and understanding of:

→ The impact of social, technological and environmental change on strategy and the functional areas.

The social environment

The social environment refers to the characteristics of the population in the markets in which a business is based and in which it sells its products.

The characteristics of the population include:

- Its size. This will affect how many people are available to buy products and to work. For example, there are more potential customers and employees in China than Iceland.
- The age structure of the population; for example, the proportion of the population under 18. The age structure will affect the types of products that might be bought and the number of people of working age. It may also affect the taxes on business.
- The family structure – for example, how many children a family is made up of on average.
- The degree of education of the workforce. This will affect the skills and productivity of the workforce.

Case study

Population changes

In the next decade India is expected to experience a population increase of around 250 million people. Much of this rise will increase the number of people in the working population. By comparison the population in China is also growing but the difference here is that this is due to ageing. Estimates from the management consultancy McKinsey are that by 2025, over 25% of China's inhabitants will be aged 55 or older, compared with only 16% in India. In India there are likely to be more than 170 million additional urban workers in the labour force from 2005 to 2025, compared to 50 million in China over the same period.

1 Analyse how the growing populations in China and India could affect businesses in those countries.

Changes in the population will affect production and demand. For example:

- With more people in the population there may be more demand for products in general.
- With more people in the population there may be a greater potential supply of labour, making it easier and cheaper to recruit in general.

- An ageing population may reduce the number of people in the workforce, making recruitment more difficult and possibly requiring more taxes on business to help fund pensions and healthcare for those who are retired.
- The family structure may influence the demand for products; a country with many young children may see high demand for toys; a country with more single people may mean food should be sold in smaller portions.

The impact of social change on a particular business will depend on exactly what the changes are and:

- What the business sells. More people in a population may mean more haircuts but does not necessarily mean more sales of luxury speedboats.
- Who it employs. More people in the population does not necessarily mean more computer programmers or architects.

Case study

Japan's ageing population

The population of Japan is ageing rapidly. Nearly 30% of the population is aged 65 or older. This proportion is expected to increase to around 40% by 2065. Businesses operating in Japan need to appreciate the impact of these changes. For some it is a threat; for example because of the challenges finding employees – but for others it is an opportunity.

Obvious opportunities are the increased demand for care services and funeral services. There is also an opportunity for tools and services that help older people live independently for longer. Companies that produce products such as hearing aids and adult nappies are also going to do well. However, there are some less obvious opportunities. For example, older people may want to keep fit, creating opportunities for leisure and gym clubs. They may also want to return to studying, creating options for schools and universities. There are also a lot of single elderly people searching for a partner, creating a growth market for senior

citizens' dating sites. Companies also need to be aware of how best to promote to older people; they often do not want to be reminded of their age, they may need clearer labelling and they may want smaller portions, for example.

1 Do you think an ageing population creates more opportunities than threats for businesses?

Changes in the social environment in the world in recent years have included:

- **Urbanisation**. This occurs when people move to the city from the countryside. It leads to heavily populated urban areas, i.e. big cities. In developing economies many people have left the countryside to move to the cities where they think they can find jobs and earn more money. The movement of people from the countryside to the city is known as urbanisation. This leads to bigger groups of people in one place. This may make it easier to target potential customers and distribute to them.
- Migration. This happens when people move between regions and countries. Immigration occurs when people move into a

country. Emigration occurs when people move out of a country. **Net migration** is the difference between the number of people leaving and the number coming into a country in a given year. Net migration into a country, brings new people and new skills. This may be welcome. However, it does increase the number of people in a country, which may lead to greater burdens on areas such as education and healthcare, and can lead to unemployment in a country if there are not enough jobs available. Immigration can be a political issue if some people feel that it creates a burden on the infrastructure of the economy.

Progress question

1   How might greater urbanisation in a country affect a business?

Corporate Social Responsibility (CSR)

One question facing managers is the extent to which they think that their business has responsibilities to society. We assume managers will want to act legally. How socially responsible a business is refers to the extent managers want to accept obligations to society over and above their legal responsibilities.

For example, a country:

- May have a law that requires businesses to pay a minimum wage to employees; a business may decide it wants to pay more than it has to.
- May have certain safety conditions for a product or working environment but a business may want to be even safer.
- May have certain labelling requirements on food products. A business may want to give more information than it has on where the ingredients are sourced and how it is produced and what it contains.

Reasons for businesses acting in a socially responsible way

Managers may decide to be more socially responsible:

- Because they understand the benefits to society of behaving in this way and want their business to have a positive impact on society. They act socially responsibly because it is the right thing to do.
- Because they know that people in society want businesses to behave this way; business that are more socially responsible may attract more customers, more employees and more investors because they are valued by society.
- Because they want to avoid unfavourable media coverage which could affect demand and the share price.

Case study

Danone

Danone is a global food business that sells its products in over 130 countries. It has sales of over 25 billion euros a year. Danone sells mainly dairy products such as Activa yogurt, mineral water such as Evian or Volvic, and baby food. Danone is aware that customers' views are changing on environmental issues and there is particular concern over the use plastic pacakaging, for example the plastic water bottles the company sells. Customers are also increasingly wary of big brands; they are more willing to try smaller local producers. Danone has, therefore, been reconsidering its mission. It now says it exists to get healthy food in as many mouths as possible and to benefit all its stakeholders rather than its main aim being to increase shareholder value. As part of this mission it has sold businesses that produce beer and chocolate as there are not good for our health.

Danone is also trying to get as many of its subsidiary businesses certified as "B Corporations" as possible.

B Corporations are certified by an independent organisation called B Lab, founded by Jay Coen Gilbert. B Corporations promote better governance and better serve the interests of workers, suppliers and wider society, in addition to investors.

Danone's managers believe that its approach will appeal to investors who are increasingly looking for good social and environmental behaviour from organisations.

1 Do you think Danone is right to focus on all its stakeholders' needs not just its shareholders?

Examples of socially responsible behaviour

▼ **Table 6.1**: Socially responsible behaviour

Stakeholder	Socially responsible behaviour may include
Suppliers	Paying a reasonable fee rather than trying to push the price down as low as possible.
Employees	Providing more benefits for staff and better working conditions than the law requires.
Customers	Providing more information about the product, what it contains and how it was made than is legally required.
Local community	Investing in local charities and facilities.

Reasons against acting in a socially responsible way

Some managers may not agree with the concept of social responsibility. This is because they may think their main purpose is to make profit and that social responsibility is a distraction that may reduce financial returns. Managers may argue that it is not for them to decide what is or is not a "good thing" to do for society, they should focus on profits and let others (e.g. shareholders) decide what they want to do with the dividends they get. These managers would argue that their role is to simply follow the law; if society feels that not enough is being done for, say, employees, the community or customers then the law needs to be changed.

If managers focus on meeting the needs of different groups this is called the" stakeholder concept"; if the focus is on profits and rewards for the owners this is called the "shareholder concept".

Case study

Samsung

In 2018 the electronics company, Samsung, announced it would spend an additional 180 trillion won ($161 billion) in areas such as research and development. This makes sense for a business which is experiencing a fall in sales of its main product – the smartphone. The smartphone has long been Samsung's cash cow but the company needs to prepare for the future. However, Samsung's announcement was also seen as part of a desire to be seen as a better corporate citizen. Its investment should generate 40,000 new jobs in the company and potentially 700,000 across the economy as a whole. South Korea's President recently called for businesses to boost growth and create a fairer society. The extra investment by Samsung is seen as a response to this announcement by the President.

1 Analyse how Samsung's decision to spend more money on research and development might benefit its stakeholders.

2 Do you think businesses should make investment decisions based on how they help society?

Activity

Research a company in your country that says it acts in a socially responsible way. Outline the actions it takes that are said to be socially responsible.

Technological change

Changes in technology are transforming the world we live in and the world of business. The products we buy and how they are bought are changing all the time. Products such as computer games, electric cars are relatively new. Buying online or paying for items with a contactless system are also relatively new. Artificial Intelligence is increasingly being used by business to make processes more efficient and to replace jobs previously done by people with computers.

Managers need to be alert to technological change because this change:

- May threaten the success of their existing products; for example, music streaming has challenged music stores and CD producers, film streaming has destroyed the film rental business, smartphones have made watches and maps less necessary.

- May create opportunities for new products that a business could make high returns from if it exploited the opportunity. For example, computer gaming is a now a tremendously successful industry that did not exist 20 years ago; sales of electric cars are booming and 3D printing will enable us to manufacture items at home.

Technological change may affect the functions of a business. For example, new technology:

- May affect the operations of the business; a business may move its sales online rather than in store; this will require a good online presence and distribution system.

- May affect the numbers and skills of employees needed; for example, staff may need training to use new equipment.

- May affect finances because the business may need to invest to acquire the technology; in the short term this could increase its borrowing and worsen its financial position.
- May affect marketing by enabling managers to gather and process data on customer habits much more effectively and enabling far more targeted promotion.

Online business

With greater use of technology by customers and improvements in access to, and speed of, online connections businesses are naturally considering the opportunities and threats this provides. Companies such as Amazon have shown the success that online businesses can have in many retail markets. Other businesses that have been successful online include music streaming (such as Spotify), film streaming (NetFlix), search engines such as Baidu, social media apps such as WeChat, price comparison sites and holiday companies (such as Expedia).

Managers must consider:

- The access customers have to make online purchases; this will depend on network coverage and download speeds.
- The cost and effectiveness of the distribution system required.
- The extent to which customers want to see or touch or try on items or talk to an assistant before buying, i.e. online might work better for some goods and services than others.
- The costs of bringing back items that are faulty or do not fit.
- Whether to retain a physical presence, e.g. to have some stores as well as an online presence.

Case study

China's digital economy

The value of China's digital economy is now over a third of the country's economy in terms of its national income (its gross domestic product). The total value of the digital economy in China reached $2.3 trillion for the first half of 2018; this represents nearly 40% of GDP.

This represents a significant shift from China's focus on manufacturing which had driven growth for many years.

Whilst very large overall, there are major differences in the size of the digital economy in different sectors in China; it is large in services but far less common in agriculture.

1   Analyse how digital developments can benefit businesses in China.

- The greater information that can be gathered on what customers want and what they search for; this can lead to dynamic pricing where the price changes regularly reflecting different demand conditions at different times and it can also lead to very targeted promotional campaigns.

Environmental issues

There has been increasing interest in environmental issues in recent years. People are concerned about what is happening to the environment. For example, there are worries about:

- The amount of pollution that affects the quality of life.
- Climate change – the warming of the environment is affecting weather patterns and disrupting regions through natural disasters such as floods.

As a result of these growing concerns there is pressure on businesses to consider the effect of their activities on the environment. In some cases, governments have changed laws to change the behaviour of businesses. For example, governments in many countries have made businesses change the way they produce to restrict pollution. Managers may also change what they produce or how they produce to limit environmental damage because they realise the damage that has been done to the world around them. They may also change behaviour to avoid criticism in the media and a loss of customers because people may switch from businesses that have a poor environmental record. Examples of how managers may change behaviour include:

- Reducing energy consumption.
- Using energy sources such as solar energy that do not damage the environment.
- Using local suppliers so that products need to be transported less
- Improving the recycling of their products.
- Reducing waste in the production process.

Taking actions that are less damaging to the environment may:

- Save costs.
- Be more appealing to some customers.
- Appeal to some investors and employees who are interested in the environmental impact of a business.
- Be the "right" thing to do by protecting the environment for future generations.

However, changing what is produced and how it is produced:

- May be more expensive, at least to change over systems and install new ones.
- May mean some products have to be changed or production stopped (e.g. diesel engine cars).
- May mean new suppliers have to be found, e.g. local suppliers to reduce the impact of transportation of materials.
- May mean new processes are required, e.g. to reduce plastic packaging.

Case study

Raya

Raya Food Industries is planning to increase its production capacity to 32,000 tonnes of food by the end of this year, compared to 12,000 tonnes last year, after adding new production lines. Raya's head of the Commercial Sector for Business Development in Raya said that the sector of food industries and agricultural manufacturing is one of the important sectors in Egypt's economy. Raya produces about 22 products, namely strawberries for export, and okra and mallow for the domestic and Gulf markets. These products account for 70% of the company's sales volume. The company is currently conducting final tests to introduce some of the new varieties of the company's product list, and has already neared finalising the specifications. These products will soon be launched in domestic and international markets.

The company does face several challenges, such as the laws governing the sector, and the increase of the prices of raw materials, especially imported ones, which affect the price of the final product, and reduces their competitive chance in the global market. Raya Food Industries started its work in 2017 with the main activities being producing and distributing fruits and frozen vegetables to the retail and food services sector, according to international standards in order to meet the needs of both the domestic and global market.

The company launched its first products in the local and global markets in June 2017 with the brands of "Lazza" and "Everest". Raya operates according to the international quality standards, and has obtained certificates such as ISO, HACCP, and BRC, which all comply with international standards. The company exports its products to several countries such as the Gulf countries, Russia, Europe, America, and Canada.

1   Analyse how the price of imported materials might affect Raya.
2   To what extent do you think the price of imported materials determines Raya's success? Assess the case for and against and make a judgement.

Progress questions

2   What is meant by urbanisation?
3   What is meant by Corporate Social Responsibility?
4   What is the difference between the shareholder and stakeholder concept?
5   What is meant by migration?
6   Explain one benefit to a business of digital technology.

Exam-style questions

Explanation and analysis

1 Explain one way an increase in migration into a country might affect businesses that operate there. (4 marks)

2 Explain two reasons why managers might decide to become more socially responsible. (6 marks)

3 Analyse the benefits to a retailer of moving its operations online. (9 marks)

4 Analyse how social attitudes to environmental issues might affect a business. (9 marks)

5 Analyse how changes in composition of a country's workforce can affect a business. (9 marks)

Evaluation

6 You own a chain of clothes shops. Should you move your business completely online? Assess the arguments for and against and make a judgement. (12 marks)

7 You are the Chief Executive of a coffee shop business. You are considering buying only Fair Trade coffee beans. This ensures suppliers get a reasonable price for their coffee but usually costs more than non-Fair Trade beans. Should you only buy Fair Trade coffee beans? Assess the arguments for and against and make a judgement. (12 marks)

7 Investment appraisal

Key terms

Investment decisions: involve a business spending money on a project now with the aim of generating returns in the future.

Investment appraisal: is where managers assess different projects to decide which ones to invest in.

Investment decisions

Part of a manager's role will be to think about the future and what needs to be done to make sure the business is ready for the future. This will involve investment decisions. Investment decisions involve a business spending money on a project now with the aim of generating returns in the future. For example, a business may invest in new machinery, new premises or new transport. These investments would be expected to bring returns in the future.

Factors influencing investment decisions

When deciding whether to invest in a project, managers will consider:

- The initial cost of it. Managers must decide if they have the funds available or if they can raise them. They must also consider how else the funds could be used to compare alternatives.

- The expected net returns each year. This will be based in forecasts of the expected inflows and outflows for a given year. This will depend on expectations about the business environment in the future: Is the market growing? Is competition increasing? All of this will affect the business confidence and therefore the willingness to invest.

- The degree of uncertainty. All projections will be uncertain but if the business environment is particularly uncertain this might affect a decision whether to go ahead.

- The risk involved if the project failed. This could include the financial risk, the risk to the brand or the legal risks if the business failed to fulfil a contract. For example, if a project failed, the business could lose the money it had invested, it might let down customers, damaging its reputation and may even be taken to court if the business fails to meet its legal obligations to supply a product. Every investment involves a risk because it is based on expectations of costs and revenues in the future and conditions may well change. Managers must consider the risk relative to the expected rewards and decide if the investment is worth it.

Methods of investment appraisal

Investment appraisal occurs when managers assess different projects to decide which one or which ones to invest in.

When choosing between projects managers will assess them to decide which projects, if any, they want to go ahead with. This helps managers to select the right projects. Assessing investment projects carefully is very important because they can involve large sums on money. Managers will want to use this money wisely because they will have to answer for their actions to investors. By carefully assessing a project managers will hope to reduce the risk of getting it wrong and choosing a project that is unsuccessful. However, this is not easy to do because investment is all about the future, and so much can change that any assumptions made at the moment may be wrong. For example, changes in exchange rates, in economic growth or in the actions of competitors can occur suddenly and unexpectedly and change the costs and revenues expected from any project.

Progress question

1   Look at what is happening in your country at the moment. Is there anything that would not have been predicted a few years ago?

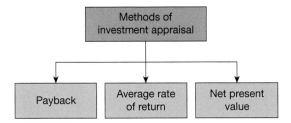

▲ Figure 7.1 Methods of investment appraisal

There are three methods of investment appraisal that managers may use:

- Payback. As the name suggests this calculates the length of time it would talk for the earnings from the project to pay back the initial cost of it.

- Average rate of return. This calculates the average profit per year as a percentage of the initial cost. This shows a rate of return which can be compared with the rates of return elsewhere or the rate of interest if funds have to be borrowed.

- Net present value. This is the most complicated investment appraisal technique. It takes account of the "time value of money" i.e. it recognises that money earned in, say, five years' time is not the same as money earned now or next year. This method accounts for the timings of payment (i.e. whether they occur in one or five years' time) to calculate whether the project is worthwhile.

The payback method of investment appraisal

The **payback** method of investment appraisal calculates the time in years and months it would take to repay the initial cost of the investment.

If two projects were identical in all other ways managers would choose the option that had the quickest payback. This is because it would reduce the risk of not being paid.

In some cases a project may be seem to be very appealing financially in the long term but if the payback is too long managers may reject it because they cannot wait too long to receive back the money that has been spent. Imagine, for example, investing in a mining project that would start to earn high returns, but only after 25 years. This might be too long to wait for some businesses. Table 7.1 shows two potential investment projects.

Link

One issue with an investment project is raising the funds to go ahead with it. This may increase the gearing of the business if the money is borrowed. Find out more about gearing in Chapter 2.

Key term

The **payback** method of investment appraisal calculates the time in years and months it would take to repay the initial cost of the investment.

▼ Table 7.1: Comparing two investment projects

Year	Project A	Project B
	net inflows $000	net inflows $000
0	−50	−50
1	20	10
2	20	10
3	20	20
4	20	100

The two projects (A and B) both cost $50,000. After two years, Project A has earned $40,000. This leaves $10,000 still to be earned (or paid back) to cover the initial investment costs. In year 3 the business earns $20,000 but only needs $10,000 to pay back the initial investment; this means only a proportion of this year's earning are needed. To calculate this proportion, you calculate how much still needs to be repaid as a fraction of the total. In this case it is $10,000/$20,000 = 0.5. This means 0.5 of the year's earnings are required. Given that there are 12 months in a year 0.5 × 12 = 6 means that 6 months earnings are needed. So, the payback period for project A is 2 years and 6 months. The **payback period** measures how long it takes to repay the initial cost of the investment.

For Project B, only $40,000 has been earned after 3 years. This means $10,000 still needs to be earned to pay back the total initial investment of $50,000. In year 4 $100,000 is earned and so the proportion of that year's earnings required is calculated by $10,000/$100,000 = 0.1 of a year. Given that there are 12 months in the year this means that 0.1 × 12 months = 1.2 months are needed. So, payback for project B is therefore 3 years and 1.2 months.

In this example project A has the quicker payback period and therefore if the speed at which the investment was recovered was the priority for the business (compared to the overall profits, for example), project A would be chosen.

- An advantage of the payback method is that it is relatively simple to calculate and understand.
- A disadvantage of the payback method is that it shows when the initial costs are recovered but does not show how much overall is earned. For example, a project may repay very quickly but then earn very little afterwards. Equally a project may be slow to payback but have high returns eventually. Project B, in the example above, takes longer to pay back the $50,000 but earns high returns eventually.

Key term

The **payback period** measures how long it takes to repay the initial cost of the investment.

Case study

GazProm

Russian energy company GazProm is investing over $55 billion to lay a new pipeline to provide gas for China. GazProm has 8,500 people working on installing a 3,000 kilometre pipeline that runs from eastern Siberia to the Chinese border.

The completion date is hoped to be December 2019. The work happens under extreme conditions involving frozen soil, rivers, swamps and freezing temperatures and even wild bears.

The project has huge risks – not just in terms of physically getting it completed but also in terms of the likely returns. It relies on demand from China for gas remaining high and gas prices holding up. It also assumes China does not seek alternative suppliers. For GazProm the project offers high returns and reduces its dependence on Western buyers. GazProm is owned by the Russian government and this project is part of that

government's desire to improve relations with China given worsening relationships with the US.

1 Explain two factors that might determine the profits made by this project.
2 Analyse the non-financial factors that might have been considered before going ahead with this investment project.

Progress question

2 Imagine there are two projects X and Y. Project X has a payback period of 2 years 6 months. Project Y has a payback period of 4 years 3 months. On the basis of this information which project would you choose to invest in and why?

The average rate of return method of investment appraisal

This method of investment appraisal calculates the average annual profit as a percentage of the initial investment.

This method has a number of stages.

1 Calculate the total profit earned by the project over its life. This involves all the net inflows minus the initial cost.
2 Calculate the average profit per year.
3 Calculate the average profit per year as a percentage of the initial cost.

For example, a company invests $50,000 in each of two projects; A and B. The net inflows are show in Table 7.2.

Key term

The **average rate of return** method of investment appraisal calculates the average annual profit as a percentage of the initial investment.

▼ Table 7.2: Net inflows for Projects A and B

Year	Project A	Project B
	net inflows $000	net inflows $000
0	−50	−50
1	20	10
2	20	10
3	20	20
4	20	100
Total profit earned	30	90
Average profit per year (profit earned / number of years)	7.5	22.5
ARR % (average profit / initial investment) × 100	15%	45%

- An advantage of ARR method is that, unlike the payback method, it takes into account the overall returns of the project and the returns can be compared with returns on other firms of investment. In the example above, the higher returns of Project B mean that although its payback is longer than Project A its overall return is higher. Taking an overview of the overall returns and without worrying about the payback, Project B would be chosen.
- A disadvantage of the ARR method is that it does not take into account when the actual returns occur. A project may have a very high average return per year but the returns may not start to occur for many years.

Progress questions

3 Calculate the payback period and average rate of return (ARR) for the project below.

Year	Net inflows $m
0	(20)
1	5
2	10
3	15
4	20

4 Comment on your findings.

Net present value (NPV) method of investment appraisal

This method of investment appraisal takes account of the "time value of money". It considers the amount of money that would need to be placed now in an alternative to the investment project (e.g. a bank) to earn the same returns as the project; the amount that would need to be placed to earn the same future returns as the project is called the present value. If this was, say, $10 million, and the project cost $7 million then the project is the better deal by ($10 million – $7 million) = $3 million. This $3 million is known as the net present value and in this case shows the project is a good deal. It would cost $3 million more to earn the same returns as this project in the next best alternative.

To calculate the present value managers need to consider how much money could grow over time; this depends on the interest rate that is expected. You will be given what are known as discount factors. These show, given an assumption about the interest rate, how much you would need to put in a bank now (present value) to become $1 in the future.

Year	Discount factor (assuming an interest rate of 10%)
1	0.91
2	0.83
3	0.75
4	0.68

The 0.91 discount factor shows that at 10% 91 cents could be invested in a bank and in one year's time it would grow to become $1.

The 0.83 discount factor shows that at 10% 83 cents could be invested in a bank and in two years' time it would grow to become $1.

The 0.75 discount factor shows that at 10% 75 cents could be invested in a bank and in three years' time it would grow to become $1.

The 0.68 discount factor shows that at 10% 68 cents could be invested in a bank and in four years' time it would grow to become $1.

The discount factor gets smaller as more years are considered; that is because if money is left in the bank for longer less has to be put in the bank initially to earn $1 in the future.

The higher the interest rate the lower the discount factors will be; this is because money will grow faster so less needs to be put in in any year.

The discount factors are used to calculate how much has to be invested now to earn given sums of money in the future. Imagine an investment of $50 million. This investment is shown below in Table 7.3. In year 0 there is an investment of $50 million. The number is in brackets to show it is an outflow.

The expected inflows are then shown for years 1 to 4.

Now consider how much would be needed in an alternative to earn the same as the project. Calculate the present value – the sum of money that is needed to be invested in an alternative to match the returns from the project. This will then be compared with the cost of the project to see whether it represents good value for money.

▼ Table 7.3: Calculating the present value

Year	Net inflow $m	Discount factor (10%)	Present value $ = net inflow × discount factor
0	(50)		
1	10	0.91	9.1
2	20	0.83	16.6
3	20	0.75	15
4	24	0.68	16.32

In the above example:

- If 91 cents would grow at 10% to become $1 then to earn $10 million we would need to invest 10 × 0.91 = $9.1 million now.
- If 83 cents would grow at 10% to become $1 in two years then to earn $20 million in two years we would need to invest 20 × 0.83 = $16.6 million now.
- If 75 cents would grow at 10% to become $1 in three years then to earn $10 million in three years we would need to invest 10 × 0.75 = $7.5 million now.
- If 68 cents would grow at 10% to become $1 in four years then to earn $10 million in four years we would need to invest 10 × 0.68 = $6.8 million now.

This means that to match all the returns of the project for the next four years you would need to invest now 9.1 + 16.6 + 15 + 16.32 = $57.02 million. This is the present value of the project.

With this sum invested today in a bank it would be possible to generate exactly the same returns as the project. The project costs $50 million; this means that the net present value is $57.02 − $50 = $7.02 million i.e. the project would costs $7.02 million less than the amount needed to be placed in the alternative to earn the same amount of returns. The project is, therefore, a good deal and the business should consider it. Whenever the net present value is positive it means the project is cheaper than the alternative – this means it should be accepted. The bigger the net present value the better the investment and the more attractive the project is. If the net present value is negative this means that the amount you have to spend on the project is more than you would need to put into a bank to earn the same returns; you should not go ahead with the project.

Progress questions

5 Calculate the payback, average rate of return and net present value of the following project.

Year	Net inflow $m	Discount factor (10%)	Present Value $ = net inflow × discount factor
0	(30)		
1	10	0.91	
2	15	0.83	
3	15	0.75	
4	20	0.68	

6 Would you choose to go ahead with project A or project B? Why?

Project	Payback	Average Rate of Return (%)	Net Present Value $
A	2 years	8%	5 million
B	5 years	14%	12 million

▼ **Table 7.4**: Summary of investment appraisal methods

Method	Measures	Measurement
Payback	The length of time it takes to pay back the initial cost of the investment.	Years and months
Average Rate of Return	The average profit per year as a percentage of the initial investment.	%
Net Present Value	The difference between the amount of money that has to be placed in an alternative investment of earn the same return as the project and the cost of the project.	$

Problems of investment appraisal

All these methods of investment appraisal:

- Are based on forecasts of expected revenues and costs in the future. The calculations will only be as good as the forecasts.

- Are based on financial estimates of the returns. They do not take into account factors such as the impact on morale or brand. For example, a new canteen may generate low returns but be good for staff morale. Investment into community projects may have little, if any, financial returns but be good for the brand and image of the business.

Non-financial criteria

There are many non-financial factors that managers may consider when deciding whether to go ahead with an investment as well as looking at what the numbers say. These non-financial criteria include:

- The ethics of an investment. Managers may avoid certain profitable investments because of the ethical issues involved. For example, some businesses would not want to buy a tobacco company or an armaments business.

- The degree of risk involved. A project may appear to have a high rate of return but if the risk is very high managers may avoid it, depending on their attitude to risk.

- The degree of business confidence. A decision to go ahead with a project will depend in part on how confident managers are about future levels of demand and their confidence in their view of costs. Managers will think carefully about the business environment. The more confident they are about the likely levels of demand the more likely they are to take the risk.

- Impact on staff. An investment in new sports facilities for staff may not be profitable directly but may help attract, motivate and keep staff.

Sensitivity analysis

Managers will be aware that business conditions can change and that investment decision are based on forecasts of future revenues and costs. Rather than assume a given set of numbers is correct managers will usually undertake sensitivity analysis. This involves changing some the assumptions and seeing the impact on the investment decision. What if costs increased by 5%? What if sales were 5% lower? By changing assumptions managers can see how sensitive an investment decision is to changes in conditions. This will help them assess the risk of any decision. The value of sensitivity analysis is that it ensures managers consider a number of different outcomes. It recognises that investment projections are just that – they are projections of what might happen and therefore it may be worth considering what if something else happens. However, managers will need to select the most likely alternatives as they cannot carry on undertaking sensitivity analysis with endless possible outcomes.

Progress questions

7 What is meant by the payback period?

8 What is meant by the average rate of return?

9 What is meant by the net present value?

10 What is meant by risk?

11 State two examples of non-financial criteria that might be considered when undertaking an investment.

Exam-style questions

Explanation and analysis

1   Explain one benefit of using the payback method rather than the average rate of return method when assessing an investment project. (4 marks)

2   Explain one benefit of using sensitivity analysis when assessing a new investment project. (4 marks)

3   Explain two factors that might be considered when a business is thinking of investing in new technology. (6 marks)

4   Analyse non-financial factors that may be considered when deciding whether to relocate a company's head office. (9 marks)

5   Analyse the risks that may be involved in a major investment into a new product. (9 marks)

Evaluation

6   You are assessing an investment project involving a new factory. Do you think that payback is a better way for you to assess this than the average rate of return method? Assess the arguments for and against and make a judgement. (12 marks)

7   You are considering a takeover and are assessing this using investment appraisal techniques. Do you think you should use sensitivity analysis? Assess the arguments for and against and make a judgement. (12 marks)

8 Choosing strategic direction

This section will develop your knowledge and understanding of:

→ Factors influencing which markets to compete in and which products to offer.

→ Strategic positioning: how to compete in terms of benefits and price.

→ The value of different strategic positioning strategies.

→ Competitive advantage.

Strategic choices are long-term, high-risk, major investment decisions that are designed to help a business achieve its objectives and fulfil its mission. Strategic decisions determine how and where a business will compete. One model that is useful when analysing the strategy of a business is known as the **Ansoff matrix**.

The Ansoff matrix

Strategic planning can be analysed using the Ansoff matrix, in terms of:

- The markets that are being targeted: are these new markets or ones the business already focuses on?

- The products being offered: are these new products or ones the business already has?

The Ansoff matrix (see Figure 8.1) shows four strategies that a business could follow:

- **Market penetration.** This strategy occurs when a business sells more of its existing products to its existing customers. It involves gaining more sales from the same target customer group and with the existing products. To do this a business may change its marketing mix to increase its market share. For example, a more effective promotional mix may boost sales. This strategy means the business is focusing on markets it knows with products it is familiar with; this means managers are taking relatively few risks with this strategy in terms of managing it. However, if the market is in decline it may be risky not to look elsewhere for other opportunities.

- **Market development.** This strategy occurs when a business sells its existing products in new markets. A new market may be a new geographical area – for example selling to Asia for the first time – or it may be targeting a new segment of the market such as younger people. The appeal of this strategy is that the business is targeting new markets which could be fast growing and have more opportunity than the existing market. It is keeping its existing products so will have experience of producing this; however, managers will not know the new market and so this will bring risks in terms of how to position and market the product.

- **New product development.** This strategy occurs when a business sells new products to its existing customers. Developing a new product can be expensive, time consuming and risky. Ideas will have to be developed and tested, then they will need to be launched and promoted. Many products fail at different stages in this process and even once launched there is a very high rate of failure in the first few months and years.

Key terms

Ansoff matrix: outlines strategic options in terms of the products offered by a business and the markets it targets.

Market penetration: where a business sells more of its existing products to its existing customers.

Market development: where a business sells its existing products in new markets.

New product development: where a business sells new products to its existing customers.

- **Diversification.** This strategy occurs when a business sells new products to new customers. For example , if a car manufacturer started to produce ice cream. In some ways this strategy is high risk. Managers will have to cope with developing new ideas and finding ways of producing these efficiently. This may involve new technologies and be difficult to get right, as Tesla have found with electric cars. Managers are also having to understand new customer needs and have to learn how to promote, price and distribute in this different setting. However, although there are huge potential risks of doing something new with new customers this may actually reduce risks for the business if it is successful. This is because the business will not be reliant on one set of products or one customer group. If demand falls in one sector it will still have sales in another market or with another product. Tata, for example, has diversified into many business areas such as tea, salt, cars and airlines.

Choosing a strategy

The choice of strategy (or strategies) by a particular business will depend on factors such as:

- **The risk involved.** In some ways aiming existing or new products at existing customers is less risky than aiming products at new customers. This is because the business will know its existing customers and how to meet their needs. However, targeting new customers can also be seen as reducing risk in that it is developing new markets. This means the business is less vulnerable to a fall in sales from its existing customers.
- **The cost.** Developing new products, for example, may be relatively expensive. The business will have to invest in market research, new product development, testing and launching the product. This is likely to be more expensive than promoting an existing product.
- **Market conditions.** If existing markets are strong and demand is growing it may be possible to keep focused on existing customers and try to sell more to them. If, however, markets are shrinking and highly competitive businesses may be looking for new markets to sell to.

> **Key term**
>
> **Diversification:** where a business sells new products to new customers.

▲ **Figure 8.1**: The Ansoff matrix

> **Link**
>
> Some of the difficulties of new product development are explored in the section on innovation in Chapter 9.

> **Activity**
>
> Research a company that you like and identify new products that it has launched in recent years. Why do you think it has developed these?

▼ **Table 8.1**: Summary of Ansoff strategies

Strategy	Comments
Market penetration	Involves increasing sales of existing products in existing markets.
	Relatively low risk as it involves existing customers and markets; the business already has experience of these.
Market development	Involves selling existing products in new markets.
	The business needs to understand the requirements of new customers and ensure that it has the resources to promote effectively, and reach them successfully.
New product development	Involves developing new products.
	This can be expensive and be quite high risk as there is often a high failure rate.
	It can take considerable time.
	However, this strategy can be valuable if sales of existing products are unlikely to grow but the business wants more sales.
Diversification	Involves creating new products and entering new markets. High level of risk as the business will be operating in more markets.

Get it right

All four strategies have appeal. What matters is what the right strategy is at any moment for a particular business. You need to analyse factors such as the risk the business is willing to take, the conditions in their existing market and the conditions in the new markets being considered.

Progress questions

1 Which of the four strategies, according to the Ansoff Matrix, are being used in the following scenarios?
- A business invests in more promotional activities to increase sales of its existing products to its existing customers.
- A business develops a new range of products for its existing customers.
- A business starts to sell its existing products in new overseas markets.
- A business develops a new product to target a market segment that is new to it.

Case study

Sonder

Mr Adam is the Chief Executive of Sonder, a producer of electric guitars and amplifiers. He took the job in 2018. Sonder's turnover is around $500 million. However, Mr Adam's aim is to reduce the number of people who give up learning to play the guitar. Around 45% of guitar buyers are first time buyers, half of them are women. Around 90% of all new players give up the guitar within the first year. Mr Adam's idea was to help more people to learn their guitar and then, hopefully, buy another. Sonder recently launched "SonderPlay"; this provides online guitar tutorials as a market penetration strategy.

1 Sonder introduced SonderPlay as a market penetration strategy. Analyse other market penetration strategies the company might use.
2 Sonder is looking for more ways of increasing sales. Would you recommend a new product development or diversification strategy to Sonder? Assess the two options and make a judgement.

Changing a strategy

A business will want to change its strategy if the old one does not work. This may be because conditions in the market have changed. For example, new competitors have come in and the business needs to change its strategy in response.

A business may also change its strategy if it sets new objectives. For example, if a business has new growth targets it may need to develop a new strategy to achieve these.

Often a new strategy is associated with a new leader. The new Chief Executive sets out to improve the business and this will often include developing a new strategy.

The challenges of changing a strategy

Any change in strategy involves risk. It involves committing resources that could be used elsewhere. Whatever the result, the question 'could more have been achieved if the resources were used elsewhere?' will be asked. A new strategy therefore needs to generate a sufficient

Link

Changing a strategy may face resistance to change. To find out more about possible reasons for resistance to change see Chapter 10.

return. A change in strategy also involves an opportunity cost – resources that are used for this project could have been used for an alternative; this means that managers will want the resources allocated to earn higher returns than they could have earned elsewhere.

A change in strategy is likely to involve:

- Investment in market research to assess the nature and size of the market. In the case of market penetration the business will want to know how best to sell more to customers; for example, are they price sensitive? Which features of the product do they value most? In the case of new product development the business will want to know what else it can offer its customers. For market development and diversification the market research will need to assess a new market in terms of the opportunities it might offer.
- New uses of resources. This might involve new processes to develop new products in the case of new product development and diversification; this in turn may require training or new staff.

Activities

Research a business that has changed its strategy in some way recently.

1   What do you think made it change its strategy?

2   What risks do you think are involved in changing the strategy?

Progress questions

What is meant by the following?

2   Risk.

3   Ansoff matrix.

4   Market penetration.

5   Market development.

6   New product development.

7   Diversification.

Case study

Competition in the market for streaming

In 2012 Netflix announced that it wanted to become bigger than HBO. At that time HBO was the leading TV and film brand and had some of the most popular programmes such as Games of Thrones. However, Netflix has been very focused in its approach. It is spending huge sums of money on developing its own programmes and is winning more awards and more subscribers than HBO.

Whilst Netflix has been chasing viewers HBO has been keen to increase profits. It has spent less money developing shows and this has enabled it to maintain good profit margins of between 30 and 40%. HBO's budget for new programming has grown relatively slowly and was about $2.3 billion in 2017; Netflix spent over $12 billion in 2018.

HBO is part of Time Warner and this group has recently been bought by AT&T. AT&T wants to reverse the trend whereby HBO has been losing market share to Netflix. AT&T is developing a new streaming subscription service with HBO at its core. AT&T is a phone business but wants its phone users to stream HBO video and HBO video users to use its phones. Disney and Apple are also launching streaming services. Disney is a major potential rival and had an extensive and very popular back catalogue of

films and success. Disney recently bought 21st Century Fox's entertainment business which it means it now owns franchises such as Star Wars and the Simpsons.

HBO now has around 100 million subscribers worldwide with around 40 million in the US. Netflix has nearly 60 million subscribers in the US and 137 million globally.

1   Explain how the strategies of HBO and Netflix have differed.

2   Analyse why HBO might have changed its strategy.

3   Do you think developing new content is the key to success in the streaming market? Assess the case for and against and make a judgement.

Case study

Coffee wars

In the 1930s Francesco Illy developed a way of storing coffee in pressurised containers as a way of keeping it fresh. The company later invented the first automatic coffee machine and then in the 1970s a coffee pod which could be placed in a machine to make fresh coffee. These pods are now in the form of aluminium capsules. The pod market has seen rapid growth in recent years.

Competition in the coffee market is fierce with companies such as Nestlé and JAB Holdings battling it out. In 2015 JAB bought Keurig, America's biggest coffee-pod system, for $13.9 billion. It has also bought Jacobs Douwe Egberts, Espresso House and Peet's Coffee. Meanwhile Nestlé has bought the rights to distribute Starbuck's products. The sales of JAB and Nestlé are about one third of the market for fresh and instant coffee, which Euromonitor International, a research firm, estimates to be worth $83 billion a year.

There continue to be a number of acquisitions as businesses seek to strengthen their position in the market.

Recently Coca-Cola bought Costa, a British coffee shop chain, for £3.9 billion ($5 billion). Lavazza bought Mars's coffee business, including its Flavia and Klix vending systems.

1 Coca-Cola has moved into a new market with a new product. Identify this type of strategy on an Ansoff matrix diagram.

2 Analyse why Coca-Cola has bought Costa.

3 To what extent do you think using the Ansoff matrix guarantees the success of a strategy?

Progress question

8 What are the labels of the axes of the Ansoff matrix?

Strategic positioning: choosing how to compete

This section will develop your knowledge and understanding of:

→ Strategic positioning: how to compete in terms of benefits and price.

→ The value of different strategic positioning strategies.

→ Competitive advantage.

Strategic positioning describes how a business competes relative to other businesses within a chosen market with chosen products. For example, does it aim to be a budget airline or a premium airline? A discount store or a more upmarket provider? The positioning of a business depends on the benefits it offers compared to rivals and the price it charges compared to others. The combination of relative benefits and price can be shown on Bowman's strategic clock.

Key term

Strategic positioning: describes how a business competes relative to other businesses within a chosen market with chosen products.

How to compete in terms of benefits and price: Bowmans' strategic clock

Bowman's Strategic Clock is a useful model that is used to look at the options available to a business for strategic positioning of a product, based on two dimensions: price and perceived value to the customer.

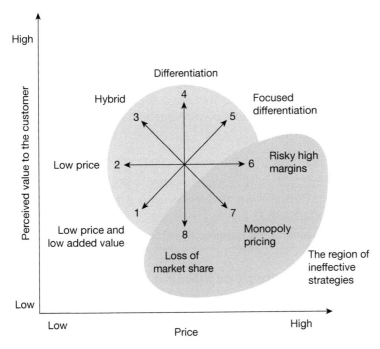

▲ **Figure 8.2**: Bowman's strategic clock

The different strategic positions include:

- Position 1: this positioning is where a business offers relatively few benefits (i.e. it is a very basic offering) but at a low price. This can still represent value for money and be appealing to customers. Imagine a budget airline; the service is basic but it is cheap so that's what you expect!

- Position 2: this is where the benefits offered are similar to rivals but the price is low meaning this is a competitive position. However, it means the business must find ways of keeping price lower than competitors so it will need some sort of cost advantage to be able to maintain this strategy and be profitable. The business may keep costs down through lean operations or scale; McDonald's matches may other fast food restaurants but keeps prices very low.

- Position 3: this is known as a hybrid strategy whereby a business aims to offer slightly more benefits than rivals and be slightly cheaper. To do this the business must again be able to find a way of differentiating whilst keeping costs lower to enable a relatively low price. For example, Ikea offers well-designed furniture at a relatively low price; it controls the design process and supply chain to keep costs down.

- Position 4: a differentiation strategy occurs when a business has a similar price to rivals but offers more benefits. This means it is a competitive offering but the business has to ensure that offering more benefits does not increase costs to such an extent that profits are affected. The danger is that the extra benefits costs so much to provide that profits are damaged.

- Position 5: is focused differentiation. This is where a very high price is charged for the benefits offered. The benefits need to be clear and well targeted to justify such a high price. This may be a strategy adopted by premium brands such as Dior.

- Some strategies would be difficult to sustain. They are in the region of ineffective strategies. For example, positions 6 and 7 are expensive for what they offer. They may be sustainable if rivals cannot compete, e.g. in a monopoly, but are not in themselves appealing to customers. For example, if the government protected an industry from foreign competition the domestic producers may be able to charge high prices. However, if competition was ever allowed in to the market the existing producers would be uncompetitive. Similarly, position 8 is uncompetitive: the business offers relatively few benefits at a price that is comparable to rivals; customers would switch if they could.

Activity

Research a market of your choice. Using Bowman's strategic clock, identify some of the major providers in this market Analyse how they have positioned themselves relative to each other.

Progress question

9 Bowman's clock analyses strategies in terms of the relative benefits and costs of a business.

How can a product that is expensive still be competitive?

Influences on strategic positioning

The positioning chosen by a business should link to the strengths and competences of the business. If the business is particularly good at keeping costs down it is more likely to pursue a low price strategy. If it has a strong brand image and an offering that is very distinct from competitors then a differentiated approach would seem to make more sense. It will also depend on:

- What competitors are doing in the market and whether the business wants to attack them head on or compete in a different way.
- What customers want.

The strategic position a business chooses is not fixed forever. Managers may decide to change the positioning of the business if conditions alter. For example, after 2008 there was a decline in incomes in many countries around the world following a major banking crisis. This led some businesses to move to a lower price positioning strategy.

Competitive advantage

A competitive advantage is what every business sets out to achieve. A competitive advantage is when you can offer better value for money than your rivals. Either you have more benefits (such as a better product design or better customer service) than competitors, which is called a differentiation advantage, or you are able to offer similar benefits at a lower price because you have a cost advantage. Having a competitive advantage will attract customers; it will help you to gain sales and market share.

However, it is difficult to sustain a competitive advantage because rivals will try and improve on what you do. What matters therefore is whether you have an advantage you can sustain. A new menu item in a restaurant may be copied easily by rivals in terms of basic ingredients, but the actual taste created by a great chef may be more difficult to copy. In this case the chef may be the key to the advantage. A particular formation in football may be easy to adopt but the style of Messi or Salah may not be; they could be the advantage. Managers will want to identify what it is that determines their advantage – is it their staff, the technology, the location? Whatever the key to the competitive advantage is, this is what managers will want to protect if they can.

Protecting a competitive advantage

The best way to protect a competitive advantage depends on what it is. In some cases it may be the people you have working for you. In this situation ensuring you offer a motivating and suitably rewarded job and a positive work environment for these employees may be the key.

However, competitive advantage may come from other areas such as:

- The brand. In this case protecting the brand values and ensuring it continues to have the right associations is important.
- The technology. If possible, a business should patent its technology. A patent provides legal protection for an invention for a number of years making it illegal for others to copy this. A patent is possible if the business can develop new and innovative technology or products.

If you are successful there will be constant pressure for rivals to imitate what you do – for example, by attracting your best staff to join them or by developing new technology to outcompete you. This incentive to innovate is one of the appealing features of a competitive market place and is much valued by consumers. For managers the pressure to innovate it means they can never be complacent.

> ### Key term
>
> A competitive advantage is when a business can offer better value for money than its rivals.

> ### Activity
>
> Research three market leaders in different markets.
>
> What do you think is the competitive advantage of these businesses?

Progress questions

10 What are on the axes of the Bowman strategy clock?

11 What is strategic positioning?

12 What is meant by competitive advantage?

13 What is meant by differentiation?

Exam-style questions

Explanation and analysis

1 Explain one benefit of a market penetration strategy compared to a market development strategy. (4 marks)

2 Explain one benefit of a diversification strategy compared to a market penetration strategy. (4 marks)

3 Explain two factors that might influence the strategic positioning of a business. (6 marks)

4 Analyse why a business might change its strategy. (9 marks)

5 Analyse why maintaining a competitive advantage can be difficult. (9 marks)

Evaluation

6 You are the Chief Executive of a business that has experienced falling profits. Do you think a market penetration strategy would be a better choice than a new product development one? Assess the arguments for and against and make a judgement. (12 marks)

7 You are the Chief Executive of a failing business. You are considering a diversification strategy but have been told it is too risky. Do you think you should go ahead with a diversification strategy or not? Assess the arguments for and against and make a judgement. (12 marks)

9 Strategic methods: how to pursue strategies

This section will develop your knowledge and understanding of:

→ The reasons why businesses grow or retrench.

→ Assessing methods and types of growth.

→ How to manage and overcome the problems of growth or retrenchment.

Reasons why businesses grow or retrench

One of the most common business objectives is growth, i.e. increasing the scale of the business. Managers often want to grow the size of their business because:

- They want it to have more power in its market.
- They want to feel safer by making it difficult for other businesses to buy them out by being bigger.
- They want to show they have achieved something as a manager by growing the business.
- Their rewards may be linked to how big the business is.

The size of a business can be measured in different ways, such as:

- The number of units sold (volume).
- The amount of the products (value).
- The market share of the business, i.e sales of the business as a percentage of the total market sales.
- The market capitalisation, i.e. the value of a company's shares.
- The number of stores.
- The number of employees.

A business grows when its size (or scale) increases.

Types of growth: organic and external

A business may grow internally or externally.

- **Internal growth or "organic" growth** occurs when a business sells more of its products; either it sells more of its existing products or develops new ones.
- **External growth** occurs when a business joins with another business. It may join together with another business to create a new organisation. This is called a merger. Alternatively, it may gain control of other organisation; this is called a takeover or acquisition.

Organic growth tends to be slower than external. With external growth there can be a sudden change in the scale of a business as it joins with another. This can bring rapid benefits but there are also challenges bringing two organisations together and coping with rapid growth.

Key terms

Internal growth or "organic" growth: is where a business sells more of its products.

External growth: is where a business joins with another business through merger or takeover.

Case study

Innocent

Innocent was started up in 2000 by Richard Reed, Adam Balon and Jon Wright.

Innocent is one of the UK and Europe's largest smoothie and juice brands, with annual sales of more than £350 million. The three founders remain on the Board of Directors but they no longer own the business. They sold the business to US drinks giant Coca-Cola back in 2013, as a result of the firm getting itself into difficulty during the 2008 global financial crisis. In the first ten years of the company it grew incredibly fast. However, when many economies went into decline in 2008, people cut back on "luxuries" such as smoothies. The position of the business was made worse when the manufacturer of all Innocent's products suddenly called to say it was closing that day due to financial problems. Then the bank said that it wanted its money back. Innocent could not pay and had to sell up. There were a number of interested buyers but the three founders chose Coca-Cola, selling the business in a number of stages. In 2013 Coca-Cola took complete control.

Coca-Cola remains committed to Innocent's ethical ideals, including giving 10% of its profits to charity. The three founders are on the board of directors.

1 Explain two factors that might influence the price paid for Innocent by Coca-Cola.
2 Analyse why the three founders of Innocent sold the business.
3 Do you think the ethical values of the buyer would have been the main factor in who the founders sold to? Assess the case for and against and make a judgement.

Progress questions

1 Distinguish between organic and external growth.
2 Distinguish between economies and diseconomies of scale.

Activities

1 Research in the news a recent takeover.
2 Produce a short report on:
   - The reasons for this takeover.
   - The possible effects of the takeover on stakeholder groups.

Retrenchment

Retrenchment occurs when a business reduces in size. For example, the bank HSBC expanded into many different countries to become a global bank. However, when it discovered that it could not be competitive in many markets overseas it withdrew from them.

Managers may decide on a retrenchment strategy:

- To avoid or stop experiencing diseconomies of scale; by retrenching the managers can return the business to a size they feel they can manage more efficiently.

Key term

Retrenchment: is when a business reduces in size.

- Because a product or market has become less profitable and so resources can be better used elsewhere.

By retrenching a business may focus on its core activities and this may improve profitability of the business.

However, retrenchment will involve job losses and so this can be resisted by employees. It may also lead to bad publicity and concerns over the future of the business because of closures.

Assessing methods and types of growth

There are several ways in which a business can grow. Each has its own advantages and disadvantages and managers must choose which ways of growing are best for their business.

Methods of growth: mergers, takeovers, franchises and joint ventures

Mergers

Mergers occur when two or businesses join together to create one new, bigger business. By merging businesses can:

- Share resources such as their research and development facilities.
- Share management expertise.
- Benefit from each others' strengths.

However, there can be difficulties with mergers such as:

- Diseconomies of scale if the business gets too big.
- A clash of cultures because of different values and different ways of doing things in the different businesses; this can lead to inefficiency.

Takeovers

Takeovers occur when one business gains control of another. This brings similar disadvantages to a merger. However, additional factors relevant to takeovers are:

- The costs of the takeover. To gain control of another business managers will have to buy the majority of its shares. To get the existing shareholders to sell their shares the price may have to rise; the company leading the takeover will pay a premium to buy the shares. This premium is a cost for the business which managers will hope to recover by an improved performance after the takeover.
- Resistance to the deal. The director of the target company may advise their shareholders not to sell. They may believe their business is better off without the control of the bidder. In this case the takeover bid is called a "hostile bid"; the takeover company will have to offer enough money and make its case strongly enough to get the other shareholders to sell.

Franchising

Franchising is one way in which businesses can grow. This occurs when one business sells the right to another business to produce or sell its product. The business that sells the rights is the franchisor. The business that buys the rights is the franchisee.

> **Key term**
>
> Franchising: is when one business sells the rights to produce or sell its products to another business.

Selling a franchise

The benefits to the franchisor of selling a franchise are:

- It raises money. The franchisor may charge an initial fee for the right to produce the product and then usually takes a percentage of the franchisee's profits; this provides an ongoing stream of income.
- It enables faster growth than might be possible without franchising. The franchisee usually provides the funds to open up their own business and this means the franchisor does not need to have the finance to pay for expansion.
- The motivation of the franchisee is likely to be higher than if they were an employee of the overall business. The franchisee will own the rights to their franchise and retain most of the profits. This motivation may make the franchise more successful than if it was just an outlet of the business.

The disadvantages, to the franchisor, of selling a franchise include:

- The business loses some control over the product and the way it is sold. Exactly how much control is given up depends on the terms and conditions of the franchising agreement. This loss of control can create risks. For example, if the franchisee starts promoting or selling the product in a way that damages the brand image. This could affect sales for all the franchisees.
- Most of the profits of franchises are kept by the franchisee.
- Risks to the brand if there are problems with a franchisee, e.g. if it does not meet required quality standards this would damage the brand.

▼ **Table 9.1**: Summary for selling a franchise

Benefits of selling	Disadvantages of selling
Raises money	Loss of control
Fast growth	Do not keep all of the profits
High sales from motivated franchisee	Risks to brand reputation

Buying a franchise

The benefits to a franchisee of buying a franchise are:

- The franchisee is buying a product that already exists and has a track record. The franchisee can benefit from the strengths of the overall brand. This is likely to be less risky than starting up on their own.
- The franchisee can benefit from the experience and training of the franchisor and the other franchisees.

The disadvantages of buying a franchise are:

- The franchisor will set out terms and conditions which the franchisee must follow. This could include how to produce the product and how to sell it.
- The franchisee will be vulnerable to anything bad that happens with other franchisees; if, for example, there is a problem with quality or customer service at one franchise it will affect the customer's perception of the brand nationally and globally.

Case study

McDonald's

McDonald's the global fast food business has many franchisees across the world. When buying a franchise the terms are the franchisee pays 40% of the initial cost for a new restaurant. This is usually a minimum of $500,000. These initial costs include pre-opening expenses, inventory, kitchen equipment, signage, the interior décor and landscaping.

When running the franchise the franchisee pays McDonald's:

* A service fee; this is a monthly fee equal to 4% of the monthly sales.
* A monthly rent.

Ongoing fees:

* **Service fee:** There is a monthly fee based on the restaurant's gross sales (currently a service fee of 4.0% of monthly sales).
* **Rent:** A monthly base rent or rent amount based upon a percentage of monthly sales is established.

The terms of a franchise for McDonald's is usually 20 years.

1 Do you think buying a McDonald's franchise would be a good investment? Analyse the case for and against and make a judgement.

Activity

Investigate a franchise business.

Summarise the potential benefits and costs of buying this franchise.

▼ **Table 9.2**: Summary for buying a franchise

Benefits of buying a franchise	Disadvantages of buying a franchise
Existing product ideas	Have to pay a fee to franchisor
Support from other franchisees	Have to follow rules of franchisor
Support from franchisor	

Key term

Joint ventures: where two or more businesses agree to cooperate in a particular area of business.

Get it right

There are advantages and disadvantages to a franchise. If you are asked to assess the sale or the purchase of a franchise you need to consider the terms and conditions of the particular franchise. How much does it cost? How successful has it been so far? What proportion of revenues would need to be paid to the franchisor?

Joint ventures

Joint ventures are when two or more businesses agree to cooperate in a particular aspect of business. For example, a multinational eager to enter a new country might link with a local firm that has expertise and local knowledge. The multinational brings the products and resources; the other firm brings local connections and insights. The collaboration may be linked to just this one region. Alternatively, there may be a venture linked to particular product or division.

The advantage of a joint venture over a merger is that the collaboration is only on one specific aspect of business that benefits both parties rather than bringing the whole businesses together. The businesses are free to compete in other areas but collaborate where it benefits them both.

Types of growth

There are three main types of external growth or integration.

* **Vertical integration**. This occurs when a business joins in the same production process but at a different stage. For example, a business may join with a supplier; this is backward integration as it is joining with a business further down the supply chain and away from the customer. Alternatively, a business could join with a distributor. This is forward vertical integration as it is joining with a business in the same production process but at a stage nearer the customer. For example, backward integration could be a car manufacturer joining with a tyre company; forward vertical integration could occur when a car manufacturer buys a car dealership business to sell the cars.

- **Horizontal integration**. This occurs when a business joins with another business at the same stage of the same production process. It means two rivals come together and gain market share; for example, two car manufacturers joining together.

- **Conglomerate integration**. This occurs when one business joins with another business in a different production process; for example, a car manufacturer and a bank. This might be to spread risk by operating in different markets.

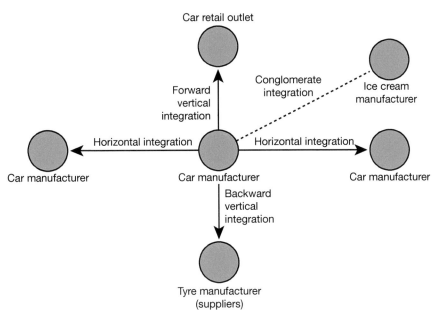

▲ **Figure 9.1**: Types of integration

▼ **Table 9.3**: Benefits of different forms of integration

Form of integration	Benefits of this form of integration
Backward vertical	Gain control of suppliers. Can control costs and quality and ensure supply more easily
Forward vertical	Gain control of distribution. Can get better access to markets
Horizontal integration	Join with similar business
	Can gain benefits of a larger size (see internal economies of scale) and market power
	Can remove a rival
Conglomerate	Can spread risks by operating in different markets

Progress questions

3 How might backward vertical integration improve the competitiveness of a business?

4 How might horizontal integration improve the competitiveness of a business?

Economies of scale

As a business grows it may experience **economies of scale**. These occur when the unit cost falls with a greater scale of production.

Larger scale can bring cost advantages. Different types of economy of scale can be seen in Figure 9.2.

▲ **Figure 9.2**: Types of economy of scale

Economies of scale may be:

- **Technical economies:** With larger scale it is possible to use production techniques that are relatively efficient but which would have a high unit cost at low level of output. A production line for a bottling plant, for example, involves a very high level of investment. If only a few bottles were produced each one would be very expensive. As output increases the initial costs of the investment can be spread over more units, reducing the unit cost. Similarly imagine a farmer with a small plot of land. If she bought a tractor this would be very expensive for every unit of farm produce produced. If, however, the farm expanded the cost of tractor could be spread over more units reducing the unit cost.

- **Purchasing economies:** These occur when a business buys supplies in greater quantities. As a more significant buyer it can probably negotiate for lower prices, pushing down the unit cost on inputs.

- **Marketing economies:** With more scale, investment in marketing activities can be spread over more units, reducing the unit cost. For example, if an advertisement cost $500,000 and only 5 units were sold the unit cost would be $100,000. If, however, 500,000 units were sold the unit cost would be $1.

- **Managerial economies:** The costs of management do not rise in proportion with the scale of the business. A manager of one person may be able to actually manage 5 people as the business grows; the management costs won't increase in this instance but the cost per unit produced will. Another managerial benefit of large scale is that the business will be able to afford specialists – for example, specialist marketing managers, specialist human resource managers and specialist financial managers. These specialists will probably make better decisions and therefore save money relative to a manager trying to do some of all these things.

Diseconomies of scale

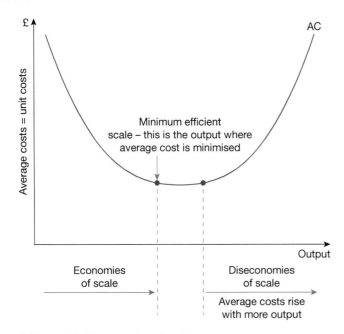

▲ **Figure 9.3**: Diseconomies of scale

It is possible for a business to get too big. This can lead to **diseconomies of scale**.

Diseconomies of scale occur when unit costs rise with more output. This is shown in Figure 9.3. Diseconomies of scale can occur because:

- There are communication problems. As a business grows it may operate in more divisions or in more regions. This means there are more people trying to talk to each other around the business. Communication flows can be slower because of so many messages from different parts around the business and this may be less efficient and increase unit costs.

- There are coordination problems. Managing a bigger organisation with more people in different departments can be more challenging. Ensuring that everyone knows what has to happen when, ensuring the right resources are in the right place at the right time can be more complex. If mistakes are made coordinating people, resources and activities this may lead to inefficiency and higher unit costs.

- Motivation. As an organisation grows individuals within it may feel less of a part of it. There may be less connection between employees and the senior management. Employees may feel less involved in the business and not feel they are recognised for what they do as there are so many people now in the business. Employees may identify less with what the senior managers want to achieve simply because they do not see them or hear from them as much.

> **Key term**
>
> **Diseconomies of scale**: when the unit costs increase with more output.

The experience curve

Business can also benefit from growing over time through what is known as **the experience curve**. Businesses that have been operating for a long time tend to be more efficient than those that are relatively new. The managers know how the market works; they know where to source supplies, how best to distribute the product, the best places to promote the product, and so on. This experience leads to better decision making and more efficiency, reducing unit costs.

Synergy

Synergy occurs when the combination of two or more businesses leads to a performance than is better than the individual parts. It is often explained by saying 1 + 1 = 3. The combined organisation does better than the sum of the individual parts. Synergy can occur in a merger, takeover or a joint venture when businesses or parts of businesses join together. For example, one business may have good links with distributors in Asia whilst another has good links with outlets in Africa. By combining, each business can benefit from the strengths of the other and both companies' products have better worldwide distribution. Another example might be a large company with funds but lacking new product ideas joining with a small innovative start up with many ideas but lacking the resources to develop them. If the two businesses come together the large company gains from the innovation of the small one; the small business gets the financial backing it needs.

Case study

GlaxoSmithKline

In 2018 GlaxoSmithKline announced its plans to split into two businesses – one for prescription drugs and vaccines, the other for over-the-counter products – after forming a new joint venture with Pfizer's consumer health division. GSK's Chief Executive said that GSK and Pfizer would combine their consumer health businesses in a joint venture with sales of 9.8 billion pounds ($12.7 billion), 68% owned by the British company.

GSK said the deal laid the foundation for the creation of two new UK-based global companies focused on pharma/vaccines and consumer healthcare within three years.

For Pfizer, the deal resolves the issue of what to do with its consumer health division, which includes Advil painkillers and Centrum vitamins, after it failed to find a buyer earlier in the year.

The new joint venture with Pfizer is expected to generate total annual cost savings of 500 million pounds by 2022.

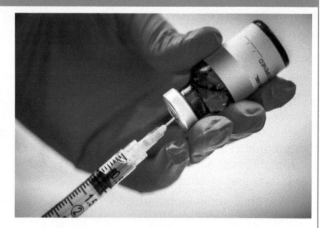

1 Explain how a joint venture might lead to a reduction in costs for the businesses involved.
2 Analyse why GlaxoSmithKline might want to split its businesses.
3 Do you think a joint venture is better way of growing than a merger? Assess the case for and against and make a judgement.

Overtrading

One difficulty that can occur with growing is known as "overtrading". This occurs when a business grows too fast and it can cause liquidity problems. In order to grow quickly the business may spend money on new resources. It will hire staff, buy premises and equipment, all of which lead to outflows of money. If this outflow is too great because growth is so fast, the business may be short of cash because it has overtraded. At this stage it may need to get financial support and grow more slowly.

Managing the problems of growth

As a business grows over time it will face a number of challenges which will need to be managed. The challenges and the actions managers can take to resolve these are shown by Greiner. Greiner's model considers some of the crises businesses typically face as they get bigger and older. As shown in Figure 9.4 this model highlights how the problems can be managed but then how new challenges may emerge.

> **Key term**
>
> **Overtrading**: occurs when a business grows too fast and encounters liquidity problems.

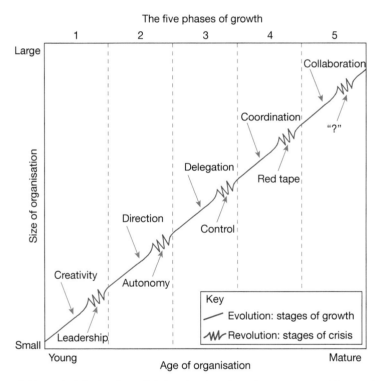

▲ **Figure 9.4**: Greiner's model showing the crises that can occur with growth

Stages in Greiner's model
Crisis 1

When organisations are small and young there is unlikely to be any formal organisational structure. It should be relatively easy to share ideas and communication should be good so at this stage the organisation is likely to be very creative. However, as the business grows, this informal approach may no longer be appropriate – new employees may need more direction and need managing. There is likely to be a "crisis of leadership"; this means that the existing leaders may not have the skills or experience to cope with the business at this stage of its development.

At some point there is a need for greater direction and leadership. This more structured approach may not come naturally to those who founded the business and who are perhaps very entrepreneurial.

At this point the business may need to appoint outside managers to run the business rather than rely on the founders. A more formal approach to management is required to steer the growth. For example, the managers may now want to formally define its mission, set out its objectives and formally define roles within the organisation so it is clear what everyone does and to avoid people overlapping with what they do. To cope with growth, managers will typically create a functional organisational structure and introduce more accounting systems and budgets.

This provides direction and control but there is little delegation. As the business grows more complex and those closer to the issues within their departments gain more experience they want to have more independence. This creates Crisis 2: a crisis of autonomy. This means that the different parts of the business are not free enough to make their own decisions; they do not have enough independence (or autonomy)

Crisis 2
Faced with a crisis of autonomy the senior managers may decide to delegate more, enabling each part of the business to focus more on its specific demands. The delegation provides more independence. It involves greater decentralisation (i.e. more decisions can be made through the organisation rather than just at the centre) and giving parts of the business the ability to make more decisions for themselves.

This delegation can lead to faster decision making but, at some point, top management may feel they are losing too much control and want to regain this. This leads to Crisis 3: a crisis of control. This means that there is not enough of an overview of what is happening in the business; the different parts of the business are operating too independently.

Crisis 3
At this stage the senior management team has to establish controls over the different parts of the business because it feels they are operating too independently. Systems that may be introduced include more formal planning procedures, greater control over investment decisions, centralising certain functions such as research and human resources and using profit sharing schemes more widely to help provide a common focus to decision making. The danger of this approach is that there it may lead to too many systems and procedures for decisions to be made by the different business units. This can cause Crisis 4: a crisis of red tape. This means that there are too many rules and procedures (which is called "red tape") which can slow up decision making.

Crisis 4
In an effort to control the different parts of the business there may be too many systems and procedures. These can get in the way of competitiveness. To overcome the bureaucracy managers may start to collaborate more directly and there may be more focus on self-control rather than imposed control from head office. Greater

Activity

Research a business that operates at a large scale.

Has it grown organically or externally?

Analyse the benefits you think it has by operating on such as scale.

discussion between the head office and the other parts of the business and a shared approach replace some of the many rules. The focus is on teamwork across divisions, up to date information and more communication between senior managers.

However, Greiner highlighted this might lead to a further crisis at some point in the future, although what it will be may vary, perhaps the impact on employees of working in such a demanding environment means some time will have to be given to employees to reflect and revitalise themselves.

The Greiner model highlights that businesses will face a variety of challenges as they grow. Whilst a solution may be found for a particular crisis any solution is unlikely to solve all the problems the business will face. New solutions need to be found to solve problems as they emerge.

The impact of growth on functional areas

The growth of a business will have an impact on all the functional areas. For example:

- Operations will need to ensure that the business has the right capacity. This may require investment or subcontracting. New production methods may become viable once a larger scale is required – for example a production line may bring economies of scale. Growth may also require more suppliers.

- Marketing is likely to have been involved before the growth. Marketing activities such as promotion and broadening the distribution channels or going online may have stimulated the growth in the first place. Marketing may now be focused on the next phase of growth, such as extension strategies for products entering the maturity phase.

- Human resources may need to recruit more staff if the business is growing organically. It may need to retain staff if new production methods are being developed. It may need to consider the organisational structure if with more products or more overseas expansion a product or regional structure might be more appropriate.

- Finance is likely to have been required to enable growth – for example to acquite a competitor or to expand outlets. Often profits fall in the early stage of growth because there are so many outgoings. Over time, in theory, the income should start to pay back the initial investments and the business will generate a good return. In the short term, however, there can be financial problems as growth can be expensive. Overtrading occurs when a business has liquidity problems because it is paying for new premises, new staff, new development and new promotions to enable growth and at this stage little is coming back in.

The impact of retrenchment on functional areas

In the case of retrenchment there will also be an impact on the functional areas. For example:

- In operations the excess capacity may be sold off or closed down so this may improve the capacity utilisation of the facilities that are left.

- In marketing the business may want to refocus its activities on its core operations now that it has closed or sold off some parts of the business.

- Financially the business may have ended production of a loss-making product or division and may make some money from the sale. It may be in a better financial position moving forwards although may have suffered in the previous periods which is why it is retrenching.

- In terms of human resources less staff may be needed due to closure. This may lead to redundancies or to staff being redeployed elsewhere in the business. This may require retraining.

This section will develop your knowledge and understanding of:
→ The value and impact of innovation.
→ Ways of becoming an innovative organisation.

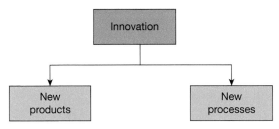

▲ **Figure 9.5**: The value and impact of innovation

Innovation occurs when a business develops a new product – this is called **product innovation** – or a new way of doing things – this is called **process innovation**. Developing the electric car was product innovation. Developing contactless shopping where you can pay with your bank card is process innovation. These two types of innovation can be shown in Figure 9.5.

New products may be beneficial because they help to keep existing customers and/or they attract new customers. New products can increase revenue.

New processes can help improve the way things are done. The business might be able to charge more for this; for example, you may be able to reserve your seats online before your flight. New processes may also reduce costs by increasing efficiency. You may be able to send bills or receipts out online rather than by post, which saves on paper and stamps.

Pressures for innovation

Businesses are subject to constant change. For example, changing customer needs, changing laws and new competitors. Managers need to prepare for and respond to this change. This requires them to innovate to survive – they need to keep developing what they offer. If they stand still whilst others innovate they will lose sales, they will have higher costs and they may struggle to survive. Many businesses have been successful for a period of time but then done badly because they failed to innovate.

Disruptive innovation

Disruptive innovation occurs when innovation completely changes an industry. AirBnB is one of the biggest accommodation providers in the world and yet it does not own one bed. When it was developed AirBnB completely changed the way that many people booked accommodation. Similarly, Uber is one of the biggest organisers of transporting passengers and yet does not own a vehicle. It completely

Key terms

Innovation: occurs when a business develops a new idea and develops it successfully.

Product innovation: develops new products successfully.

Process innovation: develops new ways of doing things.

Activity

Choose a product category such as mobile phones or cars. Summarise the innovation that has occurred with products that have been recently released.

Link

A business may differentiate itself through innovation. To find out more about differentiation as a strategic positioning see Chapter 8.

transformed the way many of us booked a taxi. Disruptive innovation can change the competitive landscape entirely. Once successful, businesses can quickly lose their markets as newcomers arrive. A famous example is Kodak. For many years Kodak dominated the camera and film industry. However, with the growth of digital cameras and then smartphones the need for film disappeared. Digital technology transformed and disrupted that industry and is in the process of changing others. In the car industry, for example, giants such as Ford and General Motors are now being challenged by producers of electric cars such as Tesla, who have changed our expectation of what might fuel a car.

Innovation and functional areas

Innovation requires change and development. This is likely to:

- Involve finance to invest in research and development. In the long run this may bring high returns but funds may be needed in the short term to get the projects happening. Some businesses may not want to spend money to develop innovative products and processes.

- Involve operations having a research and development team to come up and develop new ideas and have an approach that encourages new ideas within the organisation such as a kaizen approach.

- Require an approach to managing people that attracts high-quality employees able to develop new approaches. Managers may want to ensure that the way they manage employees encourages collaboration and the sharing of ideas rather than having people working in their own area and not sharing ideas.

- Require marketing to identify needs and wants that could be met and feedback as ideas are being progressed. Once it is decided a product will be launched the marketing team will need to promote it to raise awareness and promote the incentive to purchase.

The value of intellectual property

Intellectual property is intangible property that comes from creativity. This can be protected in law. For example, if a business has developed an innovative product or process that involves new technology it can take out a patent. A patent provides legal protection for a new invention. This means other businesses cannot copy the technology without permission. A business can sell the right to other firms to use its patent by granting a licence. Companies such as Apple and Samsung have thousands of patents for different aspects of their products. They regularly sue other companies that are trying to use this technology without permission.

Other forms of intellectual property that can have legal protection include:

- A new song, play, computer game, film or book; the rights to this form of property will be automatically protected by copyright. Anyone wanting to copy these compositions must pay a fee.

- The name or design of a product; this may be trademarked and this again prevents others copying them.

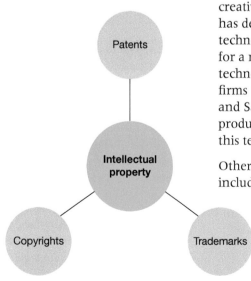

▲ **Figure 9.6**: Forms of intellectual property

All these forms of intellectual property are assets for the business. This means they can be used to earn money by selling the rights to others or, indeed, the property itself may be sold to raise finance.

Ways of becoming innovative

To become innovative a business might:

- **Ensure that the culture of the business supports innovation**. This means there is a sense that trying new ideas is encouraged and rewarded and that failing is accepted. A great deal of innovation comes after several failed attempts and so if you want successful innovation you need to accept that many ideas won't work. There is no problem with nine out of ten ideas failing, provided the tenth compensates for this!

- **Introduce a Kaizen approach**. "Kaizen" is a Japanese word for "continuous improvement". It is an approach which builds on the expertise of those doing a job. Employees are invited to work together to develop better ways of doing the work. The changes they suggest are likely to be relatively small but the kaizen approach involves employees continuously seeking to make improvements and step by step they will have an effect in the business. Each change might be small but the combined effect overtime will be significant.

- **Invest in research and development**. Innovation often needs money to support the development of new ideas. For example, managers may need to finance research and development (R&D). R&D involves spending on scientific research to develop new products and processes. Many pharmaceutical companies, for example, invest billions of dollars into research and development. Their products may take ten years or longer before being launched. If indeed it is launched. New drugs require significant testing to ensure they are safe and many products in development will not actually be able to be launched. In some cases the technology may be developed but it may not be immediately clear how to use it. In the case of Post-it notes, the inventor knew he had a glue that could enable paper to be stuck to things and removed easily, but he was not sure what to do with it until others came up with the idea of Post-it notes.

- **Intrapreneurship**. This occurs when a business encourages people within the business to be more entrepreneurial. Managers encourage staff to have their own ideas and put forward new projects and new business ideas. Entrepreneurs see opportunities, take risks and make things happen. This spirit is sometime lost in big businesses with staff doing what they are told and what they have always done. Intrapreneurship occurs when within the organisation's employees feel encouraged and supported to come up with ways of moving the business forward.

- **Benchmarking**. This occurs when managers identify an aspect of their business that they want to improve and then find another organisation that they can learn from. Managers look for the best in the world at this task and see if they can discover what that business does and then adopt similar processes. If you want to learn how best to manage queues, for example, you might benchmark against Disneyland – this means you compare what you do with what they do and try to learn from them. However, this does mean you need to find an organisation willing to share

> ### Key terms
>
> **Kaizen**: is a Japanese word for "continuous improvement".
>
> **Research and development**: involves scientific research to develop new products and processes.
>
> **Intrapreneurship**: when a business encourages people within the business to be more entrepreneurial.
>
> **Benchmarking**: when managers identify an aspect of their business that they want to improve and then find another organisation that they can learn from.

its approach and you do need to be able to implement the same approach effectively.

- **Organisational structure.** Innovation usually involves people sharing ideas and looking at issues from different perspectives. To encourage innovation you may want a structure that encourages people from different departments or divisions to work together rather than operate in their own individual section (or "silo") . Managers may want to build committees or meetings that bring together people from different parts of the business or have what is known as a matrix structure where people report to different managers (such as reporting to a manager who focuses on one product wherever it sells in the world and also reporting to another manager who focuses on one region and whatever is sold there). If a structure encourages people to stick to their role and not work with others outside it this may hinder innovation.

Case study

Spotify

In 2018 the music streaming service Spotify settled a lawsuit accusing it of infringing the copyrights of songwriters and publishers. Wixen Music Publishing sought $1.6 billion (£1.3 billion) in damages for what it argued was the infringement of over 10,000 songs.

The company, which is based in California, represents artists such as Neil Young and the Black Keys. The lawsuit was settled for an undisclosed amount.

Although Spotify has struck deals with major record labels, Wixen had accused Spotify of failing to address the claims of songwriters and publishers, who have separate rights to the compositions.

1 Analyse why the protection of intellectual property is important for businesses in the music industry.

Case study

Innovation at Tata

Tata is a large Indian conglomerate. This means it has many different types of businesses from tea to car production to insurance.

Innovation — in thoughts, processes, approaches and strategies — has become a critical factor for Tata companies as they chart a course for a future in a business world without boundaries. The objective is to consistently deliver breakthrough products and services.

The Tata group has adopted a strategy to encourage and enhance innovation across business sectors and

continued overleaf ➝

continued from previous page ⟶

companies. The key drivers are better communication and recognition of innovative ideas and efforts, facilities and initiatives that enable learning from other companies, and support for collaborative research and partnerships with academia.

Tata Group Innovation Forum

Managed by Tata Quality Management Services (TQMS), Tata Group Innovation Forum (TGIF) is a vibrant network connecting Tata companies all over the world, stimulating innovative thinking and fostering collaboration and research. The forum organises a number of events and workshops and facilitates interaction between Tata managers, innovation experts and academicians.

TGIF regularly invites academics and other experts in the field to conduct workshops and seminars which introduce new innovation concepts and tools and stimulate innovative thinking among Tata managers.

The group has set up several platforms for collaboration on technology and innovation both within the Tata ecosystem and with external organisations such as DuPont. The Tata group invests in building outstanding research facilities and forging partnerships with academic and research organisations in order to encourage creative thinking and find innovative solutions that improve quality of life.

Bringing together technologists and researchers from different Tata companies, TGIF undertook a technology mapping exercise, so that companies could gain by sharing their research and technology roadmaps, infrastructure, skills and competencies. Key innovation projects were identified where many companies could contribute. Subsequently, clusters have been formed, which are successfully working on several collaborative projects.

Facilities

Innovation centres that facilitate research, development and new technologies have been set up by several Tata companies around the world.

1. Explain the benefits to Tata of being a conglomerate.
2. Analyse the benefits of innovation to Tata.
3. Do you think more investment in innovation centres will guarantee more successful innovation for Tata?

Barriers to innovation

There are many potential barriers to innovation in organisations.

These include:

- Finance. A business may not have the funds to invest in research and development.
- A short-termist culture in the business. Managers may focus on what they can earn now rather than being willing to invest in what they might be able to develop for the future.
- A lack of interest in innovating. There may be a sense that the business is performing satisfactorily and that there is no need to change.
- A lack of the required skills. Employees may lack the skills and experience required to come up with new ways of doing things.

Link

To understand why some employees may resist innovation, see Chapter 10 on resistance for change.

Progress question

5. What is meant by intrapreneurship?

This section will develop your knowledge and understanding of:

→ Reasons for and impact of operating and trading internationally.

→ Factors influencing the attractiveness of selling to, operating in or trading internationally.

→ Factors influencing the ability of businesses to trade internationally.

→ Ways of entering international markets and value of different methods.

→ Managing international business.

Operating and trading internationally

Internationalisation occurs when a business trades with other countries. Businesses will usually want to be international in their operations and sales.

Businesses may want to become multinational because they can:

- Access resources from all over the world; this should enable them to find lower costs, better quality supplies and more talented employees than if they only operated in their only country.

- Sell to customers globally rather than only local customers; this should enable more sales because the business can access more potential buyers.

- Overcome protectionist measures by being within a country rather than exporting to it. This can allow it to avoid tariffs and quotas, and benefit from any incentives offered to foreign businesses coming into a country such as subsidies. Some governments welcome foreign businesses because they bring investment, jobs, skills and technology that the country as a whole can benefit from.

- Reduce risk by having several bases. This means if there were natural disasters or political disruption in one region business elsewhere can continue.

Multinationals

A multinational is a business that has bases in more than one country. This enables it to benefit from the best value for money resources globally and to access customers worldwide.

Multinationals may be welcomed by local businesses because:

- They bring investment to the country; this injects money in to the region which gives customers generally more spending power for local businesses.

- They bring jobs to the country; this again increases incomes and spending on local businesses.

- They can bring new technology to the country which local business can learn from and adopt.

- They can bring management expertise to the country which local managers can learn from.

- They will need supplies and so create jobs and business opportunities for local businesses.

Key term

A **multinational** is a business that has bases in more than one country.

Multinationals may not be welcomed by local businesses because:

- The profits are sometimes all returned to the home country of the multinational rather than being invested into the other country and so this may create limited business opportunities for locals.
- The jobs offered to local staff may be low level, low skills jobs.
- Little technology and expertise may be shared; it may feel as if the host country is being exploited.
- They may make it difficult for local businesses to survive. Multinationals are often powerful with a high level of resources and expertise. This may mean they can force smaller local companies out of business.

Emerging economies

Emerging economies are those that have relatively low income per person but are growing fast. Emerging economies have included the BRIC economies: Brazil, Russia, India and China. They now include many countries in Africa. These economies can offer great opportunities to businesses because of the fast growth rate. In particular they have a growing number of people whose incomes are growing, making them eager to purchase goods and services. Many businesses seeking fast growth are likely to target emerging economies.

Factors influencing business investment in a country overseas

A country will be attractive to a multinational to invest in if:

- The local government offers incentives such as lower taxes for multinationals; these would be offered to attract the multinationals to locate there and bring jobs and technology.
- The country offers particular resources such as oil or minerals or cheap labour that are appealing, relative to what is available domestically.
- The country offers a market that is attractive; for example, the number of potential customers is high and growing.
- Competition is relatively limited.

When there is investment into a country – for example, to set up a factory or to takeover an existing business this is known as Foreign Direct Investment.

Factors influencing business location and relocation globally including government actions

A country may be less attractive to a multinational to locate in if:

- It has high costs; for example, if labour or land is expensive.
- It has many regulations; this can make starting up difficult and running a business expensive.
- It is difficult to do business, e.g. due to laws or infrastructure or corruption.
- It is difficult to recruit staff.
- The market is growing slowly or declining.
- There are likely to be low returns on investment.

Activity

Research a foreign business opening up in your country. What are the reasons for it opening up? What benefits do you think it will bring to your country?

- There are high levels of domestic competition.
- There are high levels of protectionism against foreign goods.
- There are very different tastes requiring many changes to the existing product or services.
- There is a lack of experience and previous success in this type of market.
- The exchange rate is very volatile making planning difficult.
- There is political instability.
- There are high levels of corruption.

The significance for international business of differences between countries in terms of the political, economic, social, technological and competitive environments

When a business is operating internationally or considering operating in a given country it must be aware that there can be major differences in the external environment of different regions. Imagine your school set up in another country – there would probably be a different exam system, different syllabus, different times of starting and finishing school, different age at which people finish school and so on. Of course the extent of the differences depend on which country they set up in; some countries will be very similar to yours; others won't. It is the same for business – in some regions there will be major differences in the way business is done, how business is regulated, what private businesses are allowed but in others the differences may be small.

The differences in the external environment include:

- Political: for example in some countries most businesses are in the private sector but in others many are government run. You may not be able to compete in some countries. The government may also influence how easy it is for foreign businesses to set up – for example, a business may have to have a local partner.
- Economic: all you have to do is look at economic data in the news to see how different countries can be in terms of the cost of borrowing money, the unemployment rates (which will affect how easy it is to recruit), inflation (affecting costs), the growth rate (affecting demand) and the exchange rate (affecting import costs and the price of exports abroad). Differences in economies will affect demand conditions and costs and therefore the likely profits of a business operating there.
- Social: these factors can be very significant. Cultural differences can affect attitudes towards different products and what is allowed in the society (for example, alcohol and gambling are allowed in some countries but not in many others). Social factors will affect the population size (and therefore the potential demand for different types of products) and the age distribution will affect the size of the potential workforce.
- Technological: there may be significant differences between countries in terms of the technology available. For example, what is access to wi-fi like and how fast are upload an download speeds? This would affect the ease of doing business online. Technology in terms of transport (e.g. whether there are bullet trains) would affect the ease of doing business around the country. Understanding the technological opportunities will influence how a business is going to operate.

- Competitive environment: the competitive environment in terms of rivals, buyer and supplier power, entry threat and substitute threat will all vary from region to region. A business is thinking of operating in this country will want to consider these factors because they affect likely profitability. If, for example, it will rely on a few supplies who are very powerful, face major competition from existing businesses and have to sell to the government at a low price then returns may not justify the investment.

Overall, managers must consider the external environment where they operate or where they are thinking of operating because this will affect what they do, how they do it and whether the returns are sufficient. If we go back to our example of setting up another school abroad, managers might consider:

- Political: are we allowed to set up a school or do they all have to be run by the country's government? What permissions do we need to get and what rules will apply? How much of what we teach and how we teach it is controlled by the government?

- Economic: if we wanted to charge for people to come to the school, how much can families afford? Will this cover the costs? What are we likely to have to pay for the land and resources?

- Social: how many people of school age are there in the region we are considering? Are there particular religions we should provide for? Is coeducation common or should we have a separate school for boys and for girls?

- Technological: will students bring laptops to school? Will we want to make use of the internet in classrooms?

- Competitive environment: what is the number and quality of schools in the region already? How will they respond if we set up a new school?

This analysis of the external environment will influence which countries are chosen., how businesses compete and how well they do.

Case study

Merlin

Merlin Entertainment, the British operator of visitor attractions, has announced that it plans to expand its portfolio of Peppa Pig and Legoland attractions in China, following its launch in 2018 of the world's first Peppa Pig World of Play in Shanghai. The company operates more than 150 theme parks, museums, and hotels worldwide. It plans to open a number of Legoland theme parks in China.

A spokesperson of Merlin said that China is an important market for the company as it continues its strategy of geographic diversification. The company already has 11 attractions in China, including five Madame Tussauds wax museums.

The children's show, Peppa Pig, is incredibly popular in China, where it has had more than 34 billion views in less than three years.

1   Explain factors that might influence demand for visitor attractions.
2   Analyse the benefits to Merlin of having a portfolio of products around the world.
3   Do you think China is likely to be a good market for Merlin to open a Peppa Pig theme park? Assess the case for and against and make a judgement.

Case study

Smartphones

The number of smartphone users globally is expected to reach 2.5 billion by 2019. Around a third of the world's population will own one. Of the 118 elements on the periodic table 75 can be found inside a smartphone. These raw materials are extracted from the ground and shipped to refineries and factories in a global supply chain. Silicon is used to make the billions of transistors in the chips that power the phone. Gold is used for electrical wiring, about 0.03g of it in each iPhone. Indium, another metal, is used to make touchscreens. When it comes to batteries, lithium is a key component and this element is only mined in a few countries.

Until recently, Chile used to produce the most lithium in the world but now Australia has the biggest market share. The Democratic Republic of Congo, a politically unstable country with a poor human rights record, produces more than half the world's cobalt, another crucial element in smartphone batteries. Smartphone makers are under pressure to ensure their cobalt is responsibly sourced. About 80% of the cobalt used in batteries is refined in China.

Many so-called rare earth elements are also used in smartphones – in the screen, the speaker, and the motor that makes your phone vibrate. About 85% of rare earth elements are produced in China. Despite their name, rare

earth elements are not particularly rare but they are hard to extract without producing toxic and radioactive by-products. Many of the elements used in smartphones are finite resources and have no effective substitutes. Rather than digging in the ground for the elements needed for new handsets it makes sense to extract them from old phones – but only about 10% of handsets are recycled now.

1 Explain why smartphones have a global supply chain.
2 Analyse the possible challenges to smartphone producers of managing a global supply chain.
3 Do you think that all businesses need to operate internationally to be competitive? Assess the arguments for and against and make a judgement.

Key term

Offshoring: occurs when a business moves production from its own country overseas.

Offshoring

Offshoring occurs when a business moves production from its own country overseas. It moves it "off shore". It might do this because it can benefit from cheaper resources or less strict regulations if it produces abroad. A business may also shift production abroad because this helps it overcome protectionist measures. If a country is imposing tariffs on foreign products then a business may move its production to within the country to avoid these taxes.

However, offshoring can cause problems such as:

• The extra time to deliver from overseas to the domestic market.
• There may be a loss of quality as managers may find it more difficult to control production when it is overseas.

If these problems are significant, a business may decide to bring production back to the home country. This is called "reshoring". For example, some businesses have set up call centres abroad where labour has been cheaper but have found that customer service has suffered; as a result they have brought these call centre services back to the home country – this is reshoring.

International competitiveness

In recent years there have generally been more open markets, i.e. more free trade. This means there are more opportunities to sell abroad, more possibilities of buying resources from abroad or locating abroad but also more foreign competition in any market.

This means there is even greater need for a business to be competitive internationally not just nationally.

The ability to compete with businesses all around the world will depend on factors such as:

- The quality of the product and of the production process.
- The speed of delivery.
- The branding.
- The effectiveness of the marketing.
- The price relative to foreign competitors.

One important factor in international trade will be the exchange rate. This is because this will change the cost of buying products in from abroad and the price products sell for overseas. If the exchange rate of a country rises in value this means it is worth more in terms of foreign currency. This is likely to make domestic products more expensive overseas because more foreign currency is needed to convert to get the same amount of your currency. At the same time, buying products from abroad will be cheaper in your currency because your currency is exchanged for more of the foreign currency.

Exchange rates can change very suddenly – they are often very unstable – and this affects the costs of a business and the demand for the products. Exchange rates can, therefore, have a very significant effect on profits.

Protectionism

Protectionism occurs when a government protects its own businesses from foreign competition. This can be to protect jobs in industries that might face fierce competition.

Governments may use protectionism because:

- They are worried about jobs in an industry that is struggling against foreign businesses.
- They want to retaliate against foreign businesses that are competing unfairly (for example, they are deliberately selling at a loss to force domestic firms out of business).
- To put pressure on a foreign government to make it change its policies.

Protectionism may be in the form of:

- Tariffs. These are taxes placed on imported foreign goods and services to make them more expensive. This raises money for the government and encourages customers to switch to cheaper domestic products.
- Quotas. This places a limit on the number of products from abroad that can be brought into a country.

> ### Key term
>
> **Protectionism:** occurs when a government protects its own businesses from foreign competition.

Protectionism can help a domestic business to survive when facing foreign competition. This is because it may:

- Make foreign competitors products more expensive.
- Limit the number of foreign products that can enter the country.
- Make it more difficult for foreign competitors to enter the market.

The result may be more domestic demand for the protected industry's goods and services.

However, this protectionism:

- May lead to retaliation by other countries making exporting more difficult and therefore reducing sales.
- May lead to a lack of innovation as there is less competitive pressure.
- May increase costs for other industries that have to use more expensive domestic products.

Activity

Research a recent example of protectionism in the world. Why do you think this has happened? What effects do you think it will have?

Case study

VW in Rwanda

In 2018 Volkswagen announced it was opening its first car assembly plant in Rwanda. A new VW Polo costs 33 times the average Rwandan income. Most cars on the road are second-hand imports. Rwanda buys only around 3,000 new cars a year.

What is interesting about the factory is how the cars will be used. VW is linking production to a ride-hailing and car-sharing service, which will stock its own vehicles. More people will pay to use a car, it believes, than can afford to own one. Businesses and government agencies will be able to use shared vehicles. Anyone with the mobile app will also be able to call up a lift. The cars will be used for a few years, then sold into the second-hand market. The $20 million project will initially produce 1,000 vehicles, with capacity to churn out 5,000 units a year.

If it works, VW could replicate this approach. It has recently restarted assembly in Kenya and Nigeria, after decades away, and hopes to enter Ghana and Ethiopia. VW's African ambitions are similar to its decision to enter China in 1985. At the time, Chinese car-ownership rates were lower than in most African countries today. Now, VW sells over 3 million passenger cars a year there.

Some help comes from African governments, which shield producers from competition. Kenya plans to lower

the maximum age for imported vehicles, from eight years to five. Nigeria imposes tariffs of up to 70% on car imports.

Firms such as Peugeot, Nissan and Toyota have also opened new operations in Africa, often in partnership with local firms. Like VW, they are typically assembling knock-down kits, rather than building new cars from scratch. There is a long road ahead.

1　Explain why Nigeria would impose tariffs on imported cars.
2　Analyse the reasons why VW is opening up in Rwanda.
3　Do you think payback or average rate of return is a better way of assessing this investment for VW? Assess the case for and against and justify your choice.

Trading agreements

Some countries join together and form trading agreements. These are created to encourage trade between businesses in these countries. These agreements try to allow free trade between businesses in the member countries. In some cases the members agree to have common protectionist measures against non-members.

Examples of such trade agreements are:

- **ASEAN:** Association of South East Asian Nations. This has ten member states: Indonesia, Malaysia, Philippines, Singapore, Thailand, Brunei Darussalam Vietnam, Laos and Myanmar.

- **European Union:** Austria, Belgium, Bulgaria, Croatia, Cyprus, Czech Republic, Denmark, Estonia, Finland, France, Germany, Greece, Hungary, Ireland, Italy, Latvia, Lithuania, Luxembourg, Malta, Netherlands, Poland, Portugal, Romania, Slovakia, Slovenia, Spain, Sweden.

- **NAFTA:** North American Free Trade Area: the members are Canada, Mexico, and the United States.

The aim of such agreements is to encourage trade between members by making it easier to import and export. The documents needed and the checks that have to be done are simplified, and protectionist measures are removed. In some cases the movement of money between countries is also made easier as is the movement of people, i.e. people can move easily between member countries to accept jobs. This makes it easier for business to recruit the staff they need.

For those outside of the trading agreement it can be more difficult to sell into it due to protectionist measures. In some cases all members will have to have the same policies towards non-members; in other agreements each country can decide what policies they want to adopt towards other non-member countries.

Get it right

You would not be asked to name the managers of these agreements or require any detailed insight into the specific agreements. You are only required to appreciate the reasons why trade agreements exist and how they might, in general affect businesses.

Case study

Ikea

The Swedish furniture company Ikea has opened its first store in Hyderabad in India.

With a growing middle class, India could be a big opportunity for the company. Ikea's giant blue store sits on a 13-acre campus in a high-technology area of the city. The area is also home to global firms such as Microsoft, Google and Facebook.

In the past, investing in India has been less attractive to overseas companies because they could not own 100% of a business operating in India. Ikea products arrive flat packed; people then assemble them themselves. This makes the products cheaper. However, in India labour is relatively cheap so Ikea's customers are not used to assembling things themselves. Ikea is therefore working with companies to provide assembling services.

Ikea also had to change its famous restaurant product – Swedish meatballs.

continued overleaf ➝

continued from previous page ➤

Ikea's traditional meatballs are made of beef and pork. This could offend religious sentiments in India where eating pork is not permitted for Muslims. Instead there are some Indian dishes like biryani and dal makhani.

India has other challenges. Huge areas of land required for the Ikea warehouse type buildings are hard to find in most big cities. If they are available, they are expensive.

High import duties are another problem. And keeping prices low (necessary in such a price sensitive market) means it will take longer to make money back. Ikea is said to be investing $1.5 billion in India.

The investment is high and it will take some time to gain the economies of scale needed to make this profitable but Ikea is looking long term.

1 Explain two factors Ikea might have considered before deciding whether to invest in India.
2 Analyse the potential problems for overseas businesses of operating in India.
3 Do you think the benefits of selling overseas outweigh the costs? Assess the case for and against and make judgement.

Case study

Greek shipping

In 2018 President Trump of the US banned Iranian oil exports. This had a big effect on Greece. This is because Greece's merchant shipping fleet is the biggest in the world and transports a great deal of Iranian oil. Around 40% of the oil tankers moving Iranian oil around the world are Greek.

- The combined value of the Greek merchant shipping fleet is estimated at $100 billion (£77 billion), the most in the world.
- Japan is in second place on $89 billion, with China in third position on $84 billion.
- Greek-controlled ships account for 20% of global trade on the sea.
- The fleet totals 4,749 ships of more than 1,000 gross tonnage.
- Out of all these vessels, 35% are oil tankers.
- While the ships are Greek-owned, only 18% are Greek-flagged. The rest fly more than 40 national flags, predominantly the Marshall Islands, Liberian and Maltese ones. The reasons for doing this are financial, regulatory and administrative.

- The industry employs more than 200,000 people, and has remained a success while other parts of the Greek economy have been mired by the country's debt crisis over the past decade.

1 Explain why one country might ban trade with another.
2 Analyse the effect on Greek shipping companies of the US ban on Iranian oil.
3 To what extent do you think all of the stakeholders of Greek shipping companies will suffer as a result of this US ban of Iranian oil?

Progress questions

6 State two reasons for selling abroad.
7 What is meant by protectionism?

Ways of entering international markets and value of different methods

There are different ways of entering an international market and managers must consider the best way for their business.

The options include:

- **Exporting.** This occurs when a business sells products abroad from its domestic base. Exporting provides an opportunity to sell more products, which can be particularly useful if demand in the domestic market is not growing. However, exporting may require changes to the product to meet local needs and this can increase costs.

- **Licensing/franchising.** This occurs when a business sells the right to produce its products to a business based abroad. The advantages of this are that the business earns money from selling the licence or franchise and the risk of selling is taken by the other organisation. However, the disadvantage is that if sales are high the company's profits would not be as high as if it had sold them directly itself.

- **Joint ventures.** This occurs when a business works together with a local business. This can be good because it is possible to benefit from local expertise and contacts. In some countries governments insist there is a local partner if a foreign business wants to operate and so a joint venture is essential. However, the disadvantage is that profits must be shared and there may be differences in views on how to operate.

- **Foreign direct investment (FDI).** This occurs when a business sets up an outlet of a factory abroad or takes over a local business and operates directly overseas. This can lead to the highest profits (because they do not need to be shared) because the business is very close to the local market so can understand it more effectively and have less transports costs. However, FDI involves a high level of commitment and can be difficult and expensive to reverse if sales prove lower than expected.

Managing international business

When operating abroad managers must decide on how the international operations fit in relation to the domestic one. These decisions include thinking about:

- The extent to which the business responds to local conditions. One option for the business would be to sell the same product abroad as it sells domestically. The appeal of having a standardised product in every country is that it keeps operations simple. The business can produce in high volumes and benefit from economies of scale. This approach can work if customer tastes and preferences are the same around the world. Standardised global products include Bic pens, Gillette disposable razors, Nike trainers and Coca-Cola. These companies sell the same product everywhere. However, there may be pressures to adapt the product to local markets because of differences in tastes or local requirements. If you travel abroad you will know that electricity systems vary from country to country and therefore the plugs you use vary. You could not produce the same plug for every country. Similarly, if you were in the newspaper industry you would need to change your paper for different regions because people usually want local news or articles on how it affects their country. Many products may be adapted for different markets – McDonald's for example varies some of its recipes and menus for different markets. Adapting your product for local tastes may help sales but may increase costs because of smaller production runs.

- The benefits of making functional decisions centrally versus decentralising. As a business expands internationally managers may run these in different ways. One way is to let each business abroad run itself. In this case the overall company is just a collection of independent businesses. The functional decisions of what to sell, how to promote it, who to hire, how to reward staff, how to produce will be made in each region. These means that the decisions are appropriate to local market conditions but there are no benefits of being part of the overall group. The other extreme would be to make all the decisions centrally – for example, the head office decides what is produced, how items are produced, what the terms and conditions of employment are. The advantage of this approach is that the business is seen as a whole – the staff in one region may be transferred to another when needed, the profits of one country may help subsidise the start up in another, the technological developments in one region can be rolled out elsewhere. This approach has the benefit of economies of scale but may lack sensitivity to local conditions. For example, differences in local labour market conditions and labour laws may mean that HR decisions are better decentralised – how much people are paid, welfare benefits, trade union recognition and employee involvement in decision making may need to be so different that these decisions should be made locally. There are forces, therefore, for centralised and decentralised decisions and managers must decide what is best for their company. It may be that some decisions are centrally made and others are not, for example:
  - legal departments may be kept regionally because laws are so different around the world
  - marketing teams may be based in different regions because promotional campaigns have to be adapted to local tastes
  - purchasing of key supplies may be kept central to benefit from economies of scale.

Exam-style questions

Explanation and analysis

1 Explain one benefit of organic growth compared to external growth. (4 marks)

2 Explain one impact of protectionism against overseas businesses on a local business. (4 marks)

3 Explain two reasons why a business may struggle to be innovative. (6 marks)

4 Analyse the factors that might determine which country a car manufacturer decides to target for its sale. (9 marks)

5 Using Greiner's model, analyse two crises that a business can experience as it grows. (9 marks)

Evaluation

6 You have been offered a franchise in a national fast food business. Should you buy it? Assess the arguments for and against and make a judgement. (12 marks)

7 You are the producer of sports shoes. You are considering moving your production off shore. Should you do this or not? Assess the arguments for and against and make a judgement. (12 marks)

10 Managing strategic change

This section will develop your knowledge and understanding of:

→ The role and value of leaders within a business.

→ Types of leadership styles and influences on these.

Leaders

A **leader** is someone with vision. She or he has an idea of where they want the business to go. They are able to inspire and encourage others to want to follow them. A leader looks to the future and plans ahead. They focus on the long-term plans for the business, i.e. the strategy. These plans are then put into action (implemented) by others. Often people focus on their day to day job and getting this done – they focus on the short term. The leader stands back and looks ahead at where the business should be headed.

Leaders take the big decisions that determine the mission, the objectives and the strategy of the business They set out where it is headed and how it should get there.

The value of a leader is that he or she can motivate employees to want to work together towards the overall aims of the business. She or he can provide a vision that others can understand and want to follow. He or she can give them confidence in the direction that the business is headed in and make them want to part of it.

Within the business the leader is usually the Chief Executive, although he or she is supported by the managers that work for them.

Factors influencing the power of a leader

A leader will have power to get others to follow them.

This power may be derived from:

- Their charisma. Many leaders have personalities that impress others.
- Their experience and expertise. You may follow someone because you respect their views and what they have achieved in the past. You will follow them because you think they know what they are doing.
- The rewards and punishments they have available. You may follow someone because they can increase your pay, give you a bonus, promote you or allocate your uninteresting tasks. The resources available to the leader may influence how much you are willing to do as they say.

Factors influencing the styles of leadership

The style of leadership is the way in which people lead others. The style of leadership can vary considerably. The Tannenbaum and Schmidt Continuum is a useful model to analyse these different styles. This model shows a wide range of different styles used by managers.

These include:

- **Tell:** a leader tells people what they are going to do. This is sometimes called autocratic leadership.

- **Sell:** a leader sells the idea to people; she or he is still telling them what to do but is "selling the idea" to make them understand why it needs to be done.

- **Consult:** the leader asks his or her subordinates for their views and opinions. This is sometimes called democratic leadership, where managers are involving employees in decisions.

- **Delegate:** this is where the leader allows the subordinates to decide what to do.

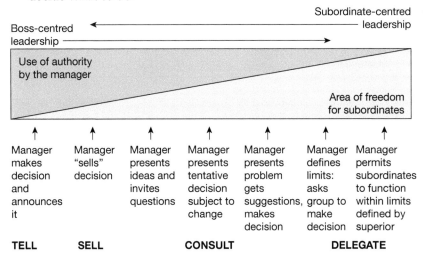

▲ Figure 10.1: The Tannenbaum and Schmidt Continuum showing styles of leadership

---

Progress questions

1 What is meant by a leader?

2 What are the sources of power of a leader?

3 What is meant by a sell style of leadership?

4 What is meant by a consultative style of leadership?

Choosing the right style of leadership

There is no one style of leadership that is "right" for every situation.

The style that works best will depend on many factors such as:

- How much time there is to make a decision. If a decision is urgent the leader may need to take control and tell others what to do.

- How experienced the employees are; if they are relatively inexperienced they may need direction and need to be told what to do.

- How much risk there is. If the leader perceives there is a high degree of risk, she or he may want to control the decision and tell the others what to do.

Factors affecting the success of a leader

The success of a leader will depend on:

- Whether the right style of leadership is adopted. If you are trying to tell people who are capable of deciding for themselves they may resent it.

- Whether others follow. Leaders need to win over followers.

▲ Figure 10.2: The success of a leader depends on whether others follow

- Whether the decisions made are the right ones.
- Whether the decisions made are implemented effectively. Effective leadership is not just about deciding the right things to do but making sure that it actually happens.

Progress questions

5   A new leader has been appointed Chief Executive of a failing multinational. What factors might influence the success of this new leader?
6   State two influences on the style of leadership used.
7   What might affect the success of a leader in bringing about a change in strategy?

Case study

Apple

Steve Jobs was the co-founder of Apple. He started in his parents' garage in 1976. He was asked to leave the company in 1985 but returned to save it from near bankruptcy in 1997, and by the time he died, in October 2011, had built it into the world's most valuable company. Along the way he transformed seven industries: personal computing, animated movies, music, phones, tablet computing, retail stores, and digital publishing. As a leader he was said to be passionate, intense, a perfectionist and impatient. He was a visionary but not easy to work for. Under Jobs, Apple had many successes including the iMac, iPod, iPod nano, iTunes Store, Apple Stores, MacBook, iPhone, iPad, App Store, OS X Lionas well as Pixar films.

When Jobs returned to Apple in 1997, it was producing a wide range of computers and peripherals. Jobs drew a grid with columns labelled "Consumer" and "Pro" and two rows "Desktop" and "Portable." He told his team members to focus on four great products, one for each quadrant. All other products were cancelled. He said that deciding what

not to do was as important as deciding what to do. Jobs thought it was important to be very focused and do what you do well rather than try to do too many things.

1   Analyse the benefits Jobs brought to Apple.
2   To what extent do you think a leader such as Jobs can determine the success of a business? Assess the case for and against and make a judgement.

Case study

PepsiCo

In 2018 Indra Nooyi stood down as the Chief Executive of PepsiCo. PepsiCo is a global soda and snack business (including Pepsi and Frito Lay) with products sold in over 200 countries and 22 brands worth over one billion dollars. She had been the leader for 12 years. Since she was first appointed PepsiCo shares have risen 78%. Indra was the Chief Financial Officer before being appointed Chief executive in 2006. Indra was said to have been a very capable leader able to keep the short-term performance of the business high whilst also focus in on the long-run strategy. Under Indra the revenue of the company increased by 80%. Indra was replaced by Ramon Laguarta who had been with the company for 22 years in a variety of senior roles.

1   Analyse why PepsiCo might have appointed a new leader in 2018 from inside the business rather than from outside.
2   To what extent do you think the success of a business such as PepsiCo can be due to the leader? Assess the case for and against and make a judgement.

Change

One of the few things that is predictable in business is that change will happen. Something, somewhere is changing in the business environment and something is likely to be changing within the business. The **pressures for change** are factors that are making change happen. The **consequences of change** are what happens as a result of change.

Types of change

There are different ways in which change may be categorised. These include:

- Internal and external change. Some change is internal; this means it happens within the business. For example, internal change might involve a change of managers, a change in the financial position of the business or a change in the success of different products. Some changes are external; they come from outside of the business. For example, external change might include changes in the state of the economy or changes in social attitudes.

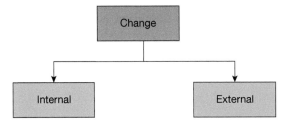

▲ **Figure 10.3:** Two types of change

- **Incremental** and **disruptive change**. Some change will be incremental; it will happen slowly in stages. For example, the population in many developed economies has been ageing in recent years. This is a long-term trend which is known about and managers have had time to prepare. Some changes are relatively minor whilst others completely change an industry (they are known as "disruptive change"). The rise of Airbnb has revolutionised the holiday industry. Driver apps such as Uber have completely changed the taxi industry. The growth of online banking has totally altered what is required to be a successful bank. Changes that alter an industry entirely are called disruptive changes.

> **Key terms**
>
> The **pressures for change**: are factors that are making change happen.
>
> The **consequences of change**: are what happens as a result of change.
>
> **Incremental change**: is change that happens slowly and in small steps.
>
> **Disruptive change**: completely changes an industry and the way business is done.

Link

Change can occur in the external environment. You can find out more about the external environment in Chapters 4 and 5.

Progress question

8   Distinguish between incremental and disruptive change.

Flexible organisations

To be ready for change and to be able adapt quickly for change an organisation will want to be flexible (also called "agile").

To be flexible a business might:

- Be able and willing to restructure. This means changing how jobs are organised depending on the current needs of the business. If, for example, a business has grown and become more global the organisation may want to have a regional structure with heads of divisions such as Europe, Africa, Asia and America. If, however, the different products it has are more significant than the differences between its regions, it may have a product structure with divisions led by a Head of Product X, Y and Z. Managers will want to choose the best way of organising their activities given the requirements of the business and its planning.

- Delayering. This occurs when layers of authority are removed. This can save money because there are fewer managers employed so their salaries do not need to be paid. It can also lead to faster decision making as information has fewer layers to go through from the top to the bottom of the organisation.

- Flexible employment contracts. This occurs when employees are hired for a specific period of time – this is a temporary contract – or for specific times of a week – this is a part-time contract.

Temporary contracts can be useful if demand is high at certain times of the year; for example, a ski resort will be busier when there is snow; a fruit picking business will be busier when the harvest occurs. Temporary contracts mean someone is employed for a given period of time. Another option is to offer employment for only part of a week; this is called part-time work. Part-time work is useful when there are certain times of the day or week when demand is high; for example, many retailers may be busier at the weekend than in the week. By employing people on flexible contracts this is cheaper than employing people all week or all year around when they are not needed for all this time. Flexible contracts allow businesses to match supply to demand when there are peaks in demand without committing to resources which will not be needed in quieter periods. Businesses may also offer employees zero-hours contracts. This occurs when employees are not guaranteed any hours of work but can be called on by managers when they are needed. Flexible employment contracts help the business to match supply to demand. For an employee it gives them the ability to work without being fully committed to the business – this may enable them to bring up a family or pursue other interests or careers. Flexible employment can, therefore, provide employees with a flexibility that may be welcomed. However, for some it may be more of an advantage to the business than the employees. Employees may prefer to have more permanent employment, a steady weekly or monthly income

▲ **Figure 10.4**: A ski resort will be busier when there is snow

and guaranteed work. For employees flexible contracts may led to uncertain earning and employment and cause stress.

- Subcontract. This occurs when a business employs other businesses to produce for it. This allows a business to accept an order even when it is at capacity. This gives a business greater flexibility because it increases its ability to meet orders. However, subcontracting brings extra costs (because the subcontractor will want to make a profit) and brings risks because it may be difficult to control quality.

Organic and mechanistic structures

Mechanistic structures exist in organisations in which jobs are clearly defined and there are very clear reporting relationships. What you have to do in your job is well defined. What you can and cannot do is set out. There are many rules and procedures. If you need a decision on something it is made clear who you ask.

A mechanistic structure typically has small spans of control. This means the number of people reporting directly to a superior is quite low. The number of levels of hierarchy, i.e. the number of levels of authority, is usually quite high. This enables managers to keep a close control on what happens because they have relatively few people to supervise.

A mechanistic structure can be very effective if a business wants a particular outcome to occur because everything is set out in terms of who does what, what has to be done and how it has to be done. If new situations occur there may be no rules or procedures in place to enable staff to respond effectively. Employees will not be used to responding to new situations and making independent decisions. In this situation an organic structure may be more appropriate.

An **organic structure** is less rigid than a mechanistic one. Employees' roles may not be so clearly defined. For example, this type of structure may involve more teamwork. Who actually leads a team will depend on the particular project and will vary from one task to another. Someone may be a team member for one task and team leader for another. An organic structure encourages people to ask others at any level in the business for advice and support rather than prescribing exactly what the channels of communication should be. An organic structure aims for creativity. However, the disadvantage may be that the outcomes are less clear and predictable so it depends what the business wants.

The differences between a mechanistic and an organic structure can be seen in Table 10.1.

Key terms

Mechanistic organisations: have clearly defined roles and procedures.

Organic organisations: are more fluid and have less fixed rules, relationships and procedures.

Activity

Choose an organisation where someone you know is employed. Talk to them about the structure of the organisation. For example, are there many rules? What's the span of control? Do you think this organisation is more mechanistic or organic? Explain your reasoning.

Progress questions

9 Distinguish between organic and mechanistic structures.

10 Identify when a mechanistic structure may be more suitable than an organic structure.

▼ Table 10.1: Summary of typical features of organic and mechanistic structures

Aspect of structure	Organic	Mechanistic
Span of control	Large	Small
Levels of hierarchy	Few	Many
Delegation	Extensive	Limited
Rules and procedures	Relatively few	Many

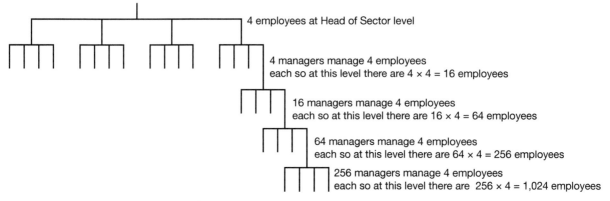

4 employees at Head of Sector level

4 managers manage 4 employees each so at this level there are 4 × 4 = 16 employees

16 managers manage 4 employees each so at this level there are 16 × 4 = 64 employees

64 managers manage 4 employees each so at this level there are 64 × 4 = 256 employees

256 managers manage 4 employees each so at this level there are 256 × 4 = 1,024 employees

▲ Figure 10.5: A tall thin organisational structure

Figure 10.5 shows a tall thin organisational structure with a span of four, where five levels of hierachy are needed to oversee 1,024 employees at the bottom of the organisation.

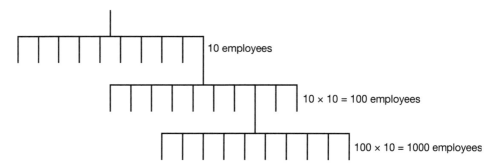

10 employees

10 × 10 = 100 employees

100 × 10 = 1000 employees

▲ Figure 10.6: A wide, flat organisational structure

Figure 10.6 shows a wide, flat structure with a span of ten, where only three levels of hierachy are needed to oversee 1,000 employees.

Managing change

Managers can just let change happen or they can try to manage it. The advantages of managing it are that:

- You can plan for it and its consequences. This means you should be able reduce any negative consequences.
- You can ensure that stakeholders know what is happening and why and are prepared for it; this can reduce fears and worries about what the change may bring.

Managing change will involve deciding:

- Who needs to be informed, what they need to know and how best to tell them.
- What resources are needed to make the change successful; for example, is any retraining needed? Is more investment needed?
- The speed of change; how fast is it needed?
- How to bring it about, e.g. should managers force it through or try and take the time to win support for it?

Lewin's force field analysis

Lewin developed a model which analysed the different forces affecting change. This was to help managers understand how to bring about more change if it is needed or how to prevent change if it is felt to be unwelcome.

Lewin identified forces for and against change. Some of these forces are called "driving forces"; others are called "resisting forces'.

The **driving forces** are those factors that make change more likely. They are factors that are pushing for a change in the present situation.

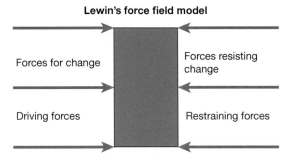

Lewin's force field model

Forces for change

Driving forces

Forces resisting change

Restraining forces

▲ **Figure 10.7**: Lewin's force field analysis

For example:

- If competitors are increasing their market share.
- If sales are falling.
- If many staff are leaving.
- If the company's share price is falling.

All of these factors would suggest something needs to change and therefore they would put pressure on managers to do something.

Resisting forces, on the other hand, create a pressure to keep things as they are and not change.

These factors resisting change might include:

- A lack of funds to finance new projects.
- Resistance from employees who want to keep their jobs as they are.

At any moment, if a situation has stayed as it is for some time it means the pressures for change are balanced by the pressures against change. However, at some point the pressures may increase; for example, the entrance of new competitors into a market may increase the pressure for change. Or the restraining forces may diminish; for example a

> ### Key term
>
> The **driving forces** are those factors in a given situation that make change more likely. They are factors that are pushing for a change in the present situation.
>
> **Resisting forces**: create a pressure to keep things as they are and not change.

> ### Activity
>
> Identify a change that has happened at a business you know. Outline the driving forces in this situation.

manager who opposed the change may leave. Change occurs when the driving forces outweigh the restraining forces.

Barriers to change

When trying to bring about change managers may face barriers from employees. According to the management writers Kotter and Schlesinger, the barriers to change from employees occur for four main reasons, which are shown in Figure 10.8.

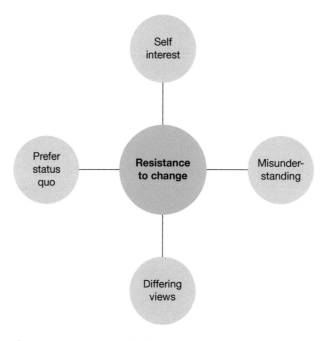

▲ **Figure 10.8:** Barriers to change

Kotter and Schlesinger's barriers to change are:

- Misunderstanding. This occurs when employees do not understand the need for change; they don't understand why it is happening so resist it.
- Self-interest. This occurs when employees feel they will be worse off because of the change; perhaps there will be job losses or a change in working patterns.
- Differing views. Employees may feel the plan for change is a bad one. They may think they have a better plan.
- Prefer the situation as it is. Employees may prefer things as they are simply because they don't like change.

Overcoming resistance to change

To overcome resistance to change managers should identify the underlying causes and adopt the appropriate policies. According to Kotter and Schlesinger there are six ways of overcoming change. These methods are:

- Facilitation and support. If employees are worried about change they may want supporting. For example, they may worry that they will not have the skills they need once change has occurred and so training may help reassure and prepare them. They may fear that

Activity

Identify a business in the news where there is a dispute with employees or a strike. With reference to Kotter and Schlesinger's model explain the reasons why employees may be resisting change.

the change will involve costs (e.g. extra transport costs to a new location) in which case financial support may help.

- Education and communication. If employees are uncertain as to why change is needed or what it will involve then educating and informing them about the change may be beneficial.

- Participation and involvement. It may help to involve employees in the process of change so they can help shape it. That way they are more likely to support it. Allowing employees to participate may lead to better ideas and better ways of doing things; it may gain the support of those staff involved which may then get others supporting it.

- Negotiation and agreement. This may help bring about change. If, for example, employees gain some rewards as a result of the change or negotiate a compromise deal this can ease the process.

- Manipulation and cooption. This involves winning people over – for example, you might offer promotion or higher pay to those who support the change.

- Coercion. This occurs when you force change through – you make it happen even if people don't agree. For example, you might threaten those who oppose with a pay cut or unfavourable tasks.

Get it right

When deciding how to overcome resistance to change it is important to identify what is causing the resistance in the first place. Is it that people don't understand the reason for change? In which case educating them might work. Is it that they do understand but realise they will be worse off? In which case trying to reduce any negative impact may be the key.

Case study

Deutsche Bank

In 2018 Deutsche Bank announced it was going to cut more than 7,000 jobs to cut costs.

Its aim was to reduce global staffing levels from just over 97,000 to significantly lower than 90,000.

Deutsche Bank employs about 66,000 people in Europe, including 42,000 in Germany, 21,000 in Asia and about 10,000 in North America. The company's Chief Executive, who had taken up the role one month before, said it would be painful but was unavoidable. The company had recently announced an annual loss of 500 million euros. It had also made losses in the two previous years. Its share price had fallen significantly in the months before the announcement.

1   Analyse why the new Chief Executive brought about these changes at Deutsche Bank.

2   If you were Chief Executive of Deutsche Bank do you think educating staff about the need for these changes is more important than negotiating? Assess the case for and against and make a judgement.

Preparing for change

Managers will want to prepare for change. Ways of doing this include:

- Forecasting. Managers will produce forecasts for sales. These may be based on past trends and/or produced through market research.

- Strategic planning: techniques such as SWOT analysis help managers to think of changes that might happen and the opportunities and threats this creates.

- Developing a flexible organisation. This is to help the business respond to change when it occurs. Flexibility may be helped by:
  - employing people on temporary or part-time contracts so they can be used when demand is high without the business committing to permanent full-time contracts
  - using subcontractors so that production can be increased if needed without committing to capacity that may not be used.
- Scenario planning. This occurs when experts are used to produce different possible situations that the business may be operating in in the future. Experts create two or three possible scenarios which describe how an industry might look in the future
- Contingency planning. This occurs when managers plan for possible unfavourable situations. For example, a business might plan for what would happen if the Chief Executive left suddenly, if a takeover bid was made or if a major supplier collapsed. By anticipating and planning for what might happen the business can have back up plans; this should enable the business to respond quickly and effectively. However, managers cannot plan for every eventuality, and planning and setting aside resources involves an opportunity cost. Managers must decide on what are the most

Case study

Shell's scenario planning

Shell has been developing possible visions of the future since the early 1970s, helping generations of Shell leaders, academics, governments and businesses to explore ways forward and make better decisions. Shell Scenarios ask "what if?" questions, encouraging leaders to consider events that may only be remote possibilities and stretch their thinking.

One scenario Shell has developed is called New Lenses on Future Cities.

Urban populations are growing and around three out of every four of us will live in cities by 2050. As cities expand, pressure on vital resources of energy, water and food increases. Across the world there are big differences in the way cities are built and run, how inhabitants move around and how they use energy. It is vital to understand more about these differences in order to make the right choices for building sustainable cities.

Research into 500 cities by Strategy&, supported by Shell, showed that cities can be grouped into six categories, or city archetypes. They analysed the six city archetypes to better understand the changing world and help create scenarios about how individual cities could evolve and become more efficient. They also examined how cities have coped with major development challenges in the past.

For example, faced with high levels of poverty and unemployment in the 1960s, Singapore has since evolved into one of the world's

most prosperous cities through smart urban planning and investment in public transport.

In New Lenses on Future Cities, Shell has identified several ways in which city leaders can help make the urbanisation process more sustainable. Effective planning to reduce the need to travel around cities, together with efficient public transport for when it is unavoidable, can make a big difference. Wider use of electric, hydrogen or natural gas-driven vehicles also makes a major contribution to sustainability, as does switching from coal- to gas-fired power generation.

1. Analyse the benefits to a business such as Shell of scenario planning.
2. You are the Chief Executive of a large global bank. You are considering investing in scenario planning. Should you do this or not? Assess the case for and against and make a judgement.

important contingencies to plan for; to do this they may consider how likely they think it is that something will occur and how serious it would be if it did occur.

Links

You can find out more about urbanisation in Chapter 6.

Progress questions

11 Explain the difference between drivers for changes and forces resisting change.

12 State three reasons why employees might resist change.

13 State three actions managers might take to overcome resistance to change.

14 What is meant by contingency planning?

This section will develop your knowledge and understanding of:

→ The importance of organisational (or corporate) culture.

→ The influences on organisational culture.

→ The reasons for and problems of changing organisational culture.

The importance of organisational culture

Organisational culture refers to the value and attitudes and beliefs of its employees.

For example, employees may believe that:

* Excellent customer service is vital.
* More profit is always better than less profit (rather than considering the impact on society of any actions).
* It is important to plan for long-term success (rather than focus on short-term rewards).
* Employees' ideas are to be valued (rather than employees are there to be told what to do).
* You should try something and see what happens (rather than wait until it is perfect before doing it).
* It is good to take risks to try and win contracts or innovate (rather than be cautious in their approach).

The culture of an organisation affects the way people behave and treat each other and others. In a culture that focuses on getting the job done no matter what, employees will tend to focus on the task and not other people; there will be little concern for peoples' welfare or general well-being. In other organisations the culture may be more people focused; this means sometimes managers may not want to push people too hard to set tasks that may be stressful.

Outward signs of culture

The culture of a business will show itself in many ways. When you visit a business, for example, you will get an immediate impression of it from many different things such as the décor of the building, the layout of the offices, the way people are dressed, what they talk about, how they talk to each other and their job titles. These all give you a sense of what people value (e.g. is formality important, is it a very serious environment, did it feel hierarchical, does the décor feel modern or traditional?). These are all outward signs of what people think – they are clues to the culture.

Influences on organisational culture

The culture of a business may be influenced by:

* The founders. The people who set up the business will have had their way of doing things and their views of what matter. This will have influenced the business when they were in control and this

will have shaped how the business developed. Years later people may still refer back to what the founders thought and what they valued.

- Recruitment and selection. The people who are recruited into the business over time and what they value will influence the culture of the organisation in the future.

- Training. If you want people to focus on customer service they will need training in this; similarly if you want them to value long-term planning you will want to ensure they understand why this matters.

- Rewards and punishments. Employees will respond to the rewards that are offered. If people are praised and rewarded for being innovative they are likely to try harder to do this; if they are punished for taking risks they probably won't. Managers should ensure their reward systems focus on encouraging the behaviours they want. Equally, employees will want to avoid behaviour that leads to punishment or prevents them being promoted to gaining rewards such as bonuses.

Progress question

15 Analyse the factors that affect the culture of a well-established business.

Why change the culture of an organisation?

Sometimes the culture may work against the business and prevent it from functioning successfully.

For example:

- Employees may be taking too many risks and this may threaten the business. In a bank, for example, staff may be desperate to meet lending targets and so may be lending to people who may not be able to pay the bank back. This could cause problems for the bank.

- Employees may be discriminating against some groups; women, for example, may not be given the opportunity for promotion or are being paid less than men for the same job. This may mean the business is failing to attract enough women and is not motivating those they do have.

- Employees may be being complacent and not focusing enough on customer needs.

- Employees may want to do what suits them not what customers want because this may be seen as too much effort.

When the culture is damaging the business managers need to change it.

Case study

Amazon's culture

Amazon describes its culture by saying:

Our Leadership Principles empower us to be owners and innovators while maintaining our customer centricity. We're willing to take risks – innovating requires failing.

1 Why might Amazon want its employees to be "customer centric"?

2 Why might Amazon want a culture where employees take risks?

3 Analyse how Amazon might create a culture that encourages employees to take risks.

National culture

The cultures of different organisations will vary. One influence on these cultures will be the country in which a business is located. The national culture, i.e. the values and beliefs of people form a particular region will affect how they behave, what they prioritise and what they value. Hofstede researched national cultures and identified a number of features of different regional cultures. These are shown in Figure 10.9. Hofstede's national cultural dimensions are key factors where there are significant differences from one region to another.

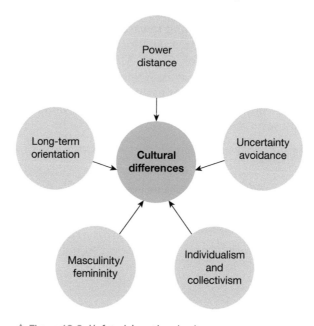

▲ **Figure 10.9**: Hofstede's national cultures

Hofstede's national cultural dimensions include:

- **Long term vs short term**: in some countries there is a focus on the short term; on others there is more long-term planning. In a business context this might affect managers attitudes to investment.

- **Individual vs group**: in some countries the performance of individual employees is rewarded. Employees will have to show how well they do on their own. In other countries team players may be valued more highly. Someone might be a "star" performer themselves but might not be good at helping the team to function well.

- **Hierarchical**: some societies are very hierarchical. In a business context this means that junior managers will be reluctant to change their bosses. In other countries the "value" of an employee will depend on what they can contribute to the task and will not depend on their age, how long they have been at the business or their job title.

- **Masculinity/femininity**: this refers to the style that individuals adopt. A "masculine approach", according to Hofstede, focuses on achievement and getting things done. A masculine approach prizes winning and rewards the "heroes" who are successful. It is a competitive approach. A feminine approach, by comparison, focuses more on the importance of cooperation and looking after others. It looks for more of a consensus rather than looking for a "winner". Hofstede describes the difference between masculine and feminine as "tough vs tender".

- **Tolerance for ambiguity**: in some societies employees will want clear directions about what to do and when. In other societies it would be more usual to have less specific instructions. This might affect how best to manage staff – if the tolerance of ambiguity is low it is important that employees have very clear instructions of what is required by when.

- An "indulgent" society enjoys having fun and enjoying life. A "restrained" society is more controlled in its behaviour and outward signs of happiness or enjoyment. Behaviour might be seen as normal in one country – for example in an indulgent society saying what you think, expressing your emotions and clearly showing if you are happy or not – and may be seen as unusual by employees from a more restrained culture.

Progress questions

16 How do you think a long-term rather a short-term culture might affect the decisions managers make?

17 How do you think a group culture rather than an individual culture might affect the way employees are rewarded?

The problems with changing culture

Changing the culture of a business can be difficult because it is trying to change what people value and think is important. Employees may resist any efforts to make them change because it challenges their existing views. How difficult this is depends on how strongly held these views are. Think about your own opinions about different things; it may be relatively easy to get you change which brand of socks you buy but it may be very difficult to get you to change your favourite football team.

How to change culture

Changing culture involves getting employees to change their values. There are different ways of doing this. Some managers may simply force change through. They may make people do things differently and hope that once they see this work they will change their views. In the short-term, employees may be doing things they don't believe in because they are being made to do them but over time they may change their minds. This approach may face a great deal of resistance.

An alternative approach may be to work to get employees to change their values and then they will change behaviour. To do this, managers may:

- Explain why a change is needed; for example, if the business is doing badly this may be a clear reason why a change in approach in required.
- Provide rewards to those who change their behaviour.
- Not reward those who do not change their approach.

Link

You can find out more about resistance to change in section 10.2.

Progress question

18 What actions might managers take to change the culture of a business?

This section will develop your knowledge and understanding of:
→ Implementing strategy effectively.
→ Matching organisational structure to strategy.
→ The value of network analysis in strategic implementation.
→ Difficulties of strategic decision making and implementing strategy.

The process of strategic planning

In theory, strategic planning is a logical, rational data-led process. It begins with a understanding of what the business is (its mission) and its objectives. Managers then analyse the micro-environment (using Porter's five forces model) and the macro-environment using PESTEL analysis. Having analysed the environment managers can produce a SWOT analysis comparing its current position and future changes in the environment (Strengths, Weaknesses, Opportunities and Threats). Managers can then select a strategy (for example using the Ansoff matrix) and implement it. Having implemented the chosen strategy managers will review its success and, if necessary, adapt it.

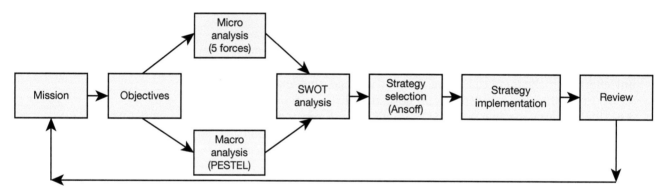

▲ Figure 10.10: The strategic planning process

Value of strategic planning

Strategic planning involves an analysis of the external environment and then compares this with the strengths and weaknesses of the business. This can help ensure the internal potential of the business is aligned with what is happening in the external environment.
A strategic plan will set out the general direction for the business. Managers of different departments then know what they are aiming for and what they have to plan for. Managers will understand what the priorities of the business are and what they can do to help the organisation fulfil its objectives.

However, strategic planning can be faulty. The plan can be wrong, in which case employees are working towards the wrong plan. In some cases, the plan might have been appropriate to start with but as conditions change it becomes out of date. The danger is that managers stick to an old plan rather than be flexible and adjust to new conditions.

Implementation of strategy

A strategy is a long-term plan. Selecting the right strategy is important because if you commit resources to move the business in the wrong direction this could put the business at risk. However, simply choosing the right strategy is not enough – it has to be put into action effectively. Many managers say that the successful implementation of a strategy is actually the difficult part. Implementation of a plan requires having the right resources in the right place at the right time. It needs a close focus on getting things done in the right way to agreed standards at a set time. Someone might be a great visionary but what is then needed are people who can make the visions happen on time.

Organisational structure

The organisational structure of a business refers to the ways in which jobs are organised. Imagine you have a football team. You have eleven players. These players can be organised in different formations – such as 4 in defence, 4 midfield and 3 in attack or 4 in defence and 5 in midfield and 2 in attack. The formations are chosen depending on who is in the team and how the team wants to play. In the case of organisational structure managers will decide:

- How to group different tasks into jobs.
- How to group different jobs.

In a functional organisational structure managers group all the jobs belonging to different functions together. For example, there is a marketing department, finance department, human resources department and operations department. The benefits of this approach are that people working in the same specialist area are grouped together and can share expertise and insights. The disadvantage of this approach is that people may become too focused on their specialist area and not consider the perspectives of the other departments enough. This is known as the silo effect, when people in different departments operate in silos rather than sharing different ideas. When considering a new product idea marketing obviously should be consulting with operations to see what is feasible, finance to see what is profitable and human resources to identify the people requirements.

A functional approach is usually adopted as an organisation starts to grow and needs to start organising different jobs to ensure it is clear who does what. It tends to be common in what are still relatively small organisations.

Key term

A strategy is a long-term plan developed to achieve the objectives of the business.

A functional organisational structure

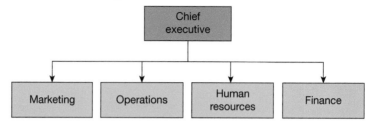

▲ **Figure 10.11**: A functional organisational structure

A functional structure (shown in Figure 10.11) is a very common way of grouping jobs, particularly for businesses that are small or medium size and focus on one main product or in one region. As an organisation expands it is likely to operate in more countries. It may export to several different countries, for example. These countries may be very different in many ways: they are likely to have different laws, different national cultures, different social and political and economic environments. The way that business is done could also vary. In India, for example, there tend to be many small shops but few supermarkets; in the UK food sales are mainly through a few big supermarkets. Given such differences between countries or regions it may make sense at this stage for the organisation to adopt a regional structure.

A regional organisational structure

In a regional structure jobs are grouped by region. There is, for example, a Head of Europe, Head of Middle East and Head of Asia. This is illustrated in Figure 10.12. Underneath these key senior managers are the different functions. The difference compared to a functional structure is that everything is organised around the demands of the region. The Asia Marketing team focus purely on marketing to Asia customers; the European marketing team focus purely on European customers. This regional approach makes sense of the requirements of each region, which may differ significantly, and there are benefits from specialising in this way because decisions will meet local requirements.

▲ **Figure 10.12**: A regional organisational structure

A product-based organisational structure

Another way of grouping jobs is around the different products that an organisation makes. This is a product-based organisational structure. Imagine, for example, that a business produces several different types of products such as food, cleaning products and soft drinks. Managers may decide to have a head for each of these product areas and then organise the functions for each one beneath this. There would, for example, be different marketing teams for each product group, different operations, different HR and different finance teams. The advantage of this is, again, the fact that people can specialise on a particular part of the business, in this case, the product. If the requirements of these products are very different – for example, they have different customers, distributors, competitors and production requirements – it may make sense to have people specialising in the needs of each product category. For example, a conglomerate business may have a food division, a home care division and a medical division in its product-based structure. A product-based organisational structure is illustrated in Figure 10.13.

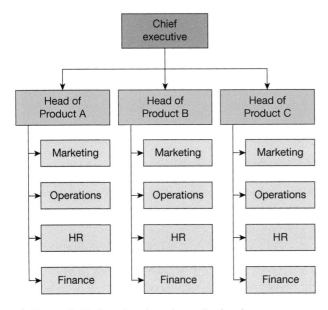

▲ **Figure 10.13**: A product-based organisational structure

A matrix-based organisational structure

Another possible **organisational structure** is known as a matrix structure. In this system employees report to more than one boss. This will help them to see different perspectives when making decisions. Imagine, for example, an industry such as the car industry. A company such as Ford or General Motors will have several brands and will also operate in many regions around the world. The marketing manager for the Ford Mondeo brand may report to the manager for Mondeos around the world, and also report to the Head of Asia who will give an overview of everything that happens in Asia – this gives an overview of how the Mondeo fits with the rest of Ford's products in that region. A matrix-based structure is illustrated in Figure 10.14.

Key term

An **organisational structure** shows how jobs are grouped within a business, for example functionally, regionally, matrix or by product.

The ability to combine different perspectives can be useful in decision making although the disadvantage is that individuals have more than one boss; it can be difficult to know whose instructions take priority at times.

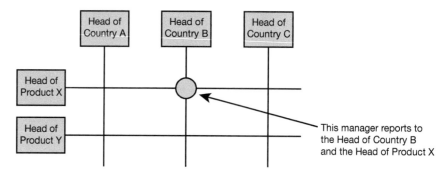

▲ **Figure 10.14**: A matrix-based organisational structure

Choosing the right organisational structure

If we go back to the football analogy it is important for a manager to pick the right formation for a given match – this depends on who you are playing and what result you are playing for – do you need to win or would a draw be enough? When choosing an organisational structure it is necessary to pick the right structure for the given conditions. For example, a business with very different products may want a product approach. A business that operates in very different regions may want a regional approach. The structure needs to fit the specific demands of the business.

Progress question

21 Analyse the advantages and disadvantages of a functional organisational structure.

Implementing a strategy

Developing the right strategy is important. A business needs to be competing in the right markets with the right products. It needs to be positioned appropriately. However, many managers say the real challenge is not selecting the strategy – it is implementing it effectively and making sure it happens. This means making sure you have everything such as money, the people, the commitment, the shared understanding of what is needed and the technology in the right place at the right time.

The effective implementation of a strategy is likely to involve:

- **Good leadership**: a leader (or team of leaders such as senior managers) needs to provide a clear direction for the business. They need to set out what the business is and what it wants to be. They inspire and motivate employees. They coordinate the actions of employees so they are all working towards the same goals.

  The leader will:

  – set clear objectives for everyone and communicate these clearly

  – coordinate all the resources to make sure they are ready as and when they are needed and are of the right quality

- monitor progress to ensure nothing is going wrong and if it is, working out how to fix it.
- **Effective communications**: it is important that the targets and the strategy are communicated effectively so that employees know what is expected of them, what they have to do when and why. Progress needs to be monitored closely and if there is any problem this needs to be shared so plans can be adjusted accordingly.
- **The organisational structure** will need to be appropriate for the strategy. The structure refers to how jobs are grouped together.

Progress questions

22 Analyse how a leader can help a strategy to be successful.
23 Analyse why good communication is important for a strategy to be successful.
24 Analyse why the right organisational structure is important for a strategy to be successful.

Network analysis

Managers will use a variety of techniques and technologies to ensure people can track progress and take actions if necessary. One planning tool is known as "**network analysis**". Network analysis is a visual representation of the different activities involved in a project, the order they must be carried out in and the time they take.

Network analysis is used to find the quickest way a project can be completed. It can be used to help plan and coordinate the development of major projects such as construction works.

Managers will:

- Identify all the activities that need to take place for the project.
- Identify which activities have to happen in a particular order (e.g. some activities may only be possible if something else has been completed) and which can be carried out simultaneously (i.e. it may be possible to carry out one activity at the same time as another activity).
- Estimate how long each activity will take. Note that how long an activity takes may depend on how many resources are allocated to it and the quality standards set for it. With more resources and a willingness to accept lower standards it is possible an activity could be completed faster.

From this information it is possible to build a network diagram showing the activities to be undertaken and the order they are to be carried out in. It will be possible to identify the quickest way a project can be completed.

Managers can also work out for each activity:

- The **Earliest Start Time** (EST): this is the earliest that a particular activity can start. For example if one activity starts on Day 0 and takes 4 days then the EST of the next activity is Day 4. Knowing the EST of any activity is important because it can show when materials can be ordered to arrive. If managers want to adopt a

> **Key term**
>
> **Network analysis**: is a visual representation of the different activities involved in a project, the order they must be carried out in and the time they take.

just-in-time approach they will not want materials to arrive before the EST because they will simply sit there and take up space. Getting materials to arrive just when they are needed can therefore help cashflow.

- The **Latest Finish Time** (LFT): this is the latest an activity could be finished for the project to be completed in the shortest possible time possible. If one activity has to finish on Day 12 for the whole project to finish on time and it takes 8 days to do then the LFT of the activity before is day 4. If the activity finished later than this it will have a knock-on effect and delay the project as a whole.

- **Total float time**. This is how long an activity could overrun without delaying the project as a whole. On some activities there will be spare time – for example, it may be that an activity could take 2 days longer than expected and it may still not have any impact because it was not critical for this activity to be completed in the shortest time possible. Knowing how much float an activity has is important as managers can determine how serious any overrun is. For example, if an activity is going to take 4 days longer than originally expected but the float is 6 days, this is not a problem. If, however, a project is going to take 4 days longer than originally expected and the float was only 2 days this is a problem and will delay the project as a whole. Managers must analyse the impact of this.

Some activities will have a float time. If the float time is 0 it means these activities are "critical"; if they are delayed at all this will delay the project as a whole. Managers will prioritise critical activities to try and ensure nothing delays them.

The total float time is calculated by:

Latest Finish Time – duration of the activity – Earliest Start Time

For example, an activity takes 5 days; it can be started on day 3 and needs to be finished by day 12. Total float time = 12 – 5 – 3 = 4 days; this activity could overrun by 4 days and the project as a whole would still be on time.

By comparison, if an activity takes 5 days; it can be started on day 3 and needs to be finished by day 8.

Total float time = 8 – 5 – 3 = 0 days; this activity cannot overrun at all or the whole project will be delayed. This is a **critical activity**.

Progress question

25 Calculate the float times for the activities below.

Activities	EST (days)	Duration (days)	LFT (days)
A	2	5	12
B	4	3	8
C	5	6	11
D	2	1	10

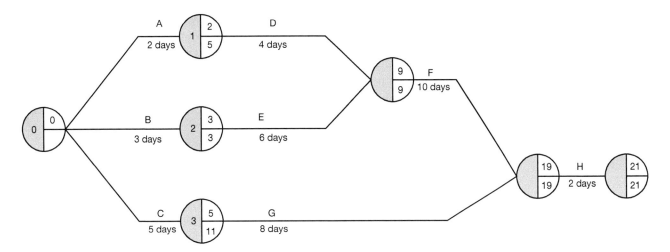

▲ **Figure 10.15**: Example of network analysis

A network diagram immediately provides a great deal of information. From Figure 10.15 we can see:

- There are 8 activities (A to H). Each activity is shown by a line. The label for the activity is placed above the line. At the start and end of each activity is circle; this is called a node.

- The duration of each activity; this is shown below the line. (e.g. activity A last 2 days, B last 3 days).

- The order that activities can be carried out. Activities A, B and C can be carried out simultaneously; that is why they all start from the same node and are in parallel. However, activity D must follow A, E must follow B, G must follow C, etc.

- Each node is numbered on the left hand side. In this case from 1 to 8; this is simply to make identifying the node easier. On the right hand side of the node the semicircle is divided into two parts:

  - the top part shows the Earliest Start Time; this is the earliest that the following activity can begin. It begins at 0 for node 1 because this is when the project can begin. We then work from left to right to calculate the EST for the following activities. For activity D, for example the EST is 2. This is because A can start at 0; it takes 2 days so we add this on and get the EST of 2 for D. Similarly the EST for E is 3. This is because B can start at 0; with a 3 days duration E can start on day 3. Note that the EST for F is day 10. D can start on day 2 and takes 4 days so we can move on from here on day 6; however, E can start on day 3 and takes 6 days so we will only be ready to move on here on day 9; to start activity F we need to wait for both D and F to be completed and so F can only begin on day 9. To calculate ESTs we therefore take the EST of the activity before and add on the duration; if we are waiting for two or more activities we have to wait for the last one to be finished so we take the biggest number

  - the bottom part of the node shows the Latest Finish Time of the activity before. You go to the end of the activity and look at the bottom right of the node at the end. For example, the LFT for A is 5, for D is 9, for F is 19. To calculate the LFTs we start at the end of the activity. We know the final EST is 21 days. This is when the whole project can be completed. This is therefore the

LFT for activity H so we put this in the bottom right of the final node. We then work backwards from right to left. If H can finish on day 21 and it takes 2 days, this means the activities before have an LFT of 21−2 = 19 days. If F has an LFT 19 days and it take 10 days then the LFT of the activities before is 19−10 = 9 days. So to calculate the LFT of an activity we use:

LFT of next activity − duration.

- If we look at what LFT to put in the first node we have three choices, A must finish by day 5 and has a duration of 2 days so the LFT of the preceding activity for this could be 3 days; for B it would be 0 and for C it could be 11−5 = 6 days. Given that all three need to happen simultaneously the LFT must be smallest number; if it was any later than that one of the activities would not be finished in time. For example, if we put an LFT of 6 in node 1 this would mean that B would complete in 6 plus 3 day duration = 9; this is too late. We therefore put an LFT of 0 in node 1. When calculating LFTs if we have a choice of more than one number we always put the lowest.

- We can now calculate the total float time of any activity using: Latest Finish Time − duration − Earliest Start Time.

▼ Table 10.2: Total float times

Activity	LFT	Duration	EST	Total Float = LFT−duration−EST
A	5	2	0	3
B	3	3	0	0
C	11	5	0	6
D	9	4	2	3
E	9	6	3	0
F	19	10	9	0
G	19	8	5	6
H	21	2	19	0

- From this we can see that activities B, E, F and H have no total float. These are critical activities. If there is a delay on any of these activities the whole project will be delayed and take longer than 21 days. The path of activities BEFH is called the critical path. Managers will prioritise these activities to make sure they are completed on time.

Progress question

26 Look at the network analysis above.
    Complete the ESTs and LFTs for each activity.
    How long in total will the project take to complete?
    What is the critical path?

Get it right

If an activity takes longer than originally estimated this does not mean that network analysis is a waste of time; the whole point of network analysis is to be able to calculate the effect of any delay and react accordingly.

The value of network analysis

Network analysis is a planning tool. It highlights what needs to be done when. This is important for ordering supplies and organising people and other resources. By organising the activities in the best way possible the project can be completed in the shortest time possible. The network analysis helps managers identify the critical activities and focus on making sure they are completed on time.

Of course, not everything will go according to plan. Some activities may overrun due to delays. In this situation the network analysis shows how significant a problem this is and managers can take appropriate action. If the project is going to miss its completion date, it is better to know as early as possible.

Case study

China–Pakistan Economic Corridor (CPEC)

The China–Pakistan Economic Corridor (CPEC) is an enormous project to bring these two countries closer together economically and improve the flows of trade. It is actually 157 different construction projects to link the two countries by creating transport links and establishing industrial areas. It has involved massive spending and building work which has helped stimulate Pakistan's economy.

The corridor construction has created nearly 60,000 direct jobs in Pakistan. It is expected to create 700,000 jobs in the country by 2030. If related industries are counted, at least 3.5 million jobs will be created, benefiting millions of families.

1 Analyse how network analysis could help businesses involved in the construction of the China-Pakistan Economic Corridor.

The value of strategic planning

Strategic planning involves developing and implementing the strategy or strategies necessary to achieve the business objectives. Managers will consider:

- What the business wants to achieve and when.
- The internal strengths and weaknesses of the business.
- The future opportunities and threats created by the external environment.

Managers will then develop a strategy. This could, for example, focus on building on the strategy to explain the opportunities the business faces or it might try to protect the business from future threats.

The process of strategic planning is valuable because managers:

- Have to look internally and externally to understand what the best strategy would be.
- Have to consider how to implement the plan; this involves considering the resources needed, the opportunity cost, how to organise activities and how to manage the people involved.

However, strategic planning does not guarantee success and many strategies fail.

Why do strategies fail?

Strategies fail because:

- It was the wrong strategy in the first place. Managers may have failed to gain enough information or misinterpreted the information they had and chose the wrong route. For example, they carried on producing diesel cars when they should have been exploring electric.
- The strategy was implemented badly. For example, projects overran or the quality of the implementation was poor.
- The conditions changed so that the original strategy became inappropriate.

Activity

Research a business that has closed recently. Can you identify why it failed? Why did its strategy go wrong do you think?

Key term

Strategic drift: occurs when the current strategy of the business is no longer suitable for the business conditions.

Strategic drift

Strategic drift occurs when the current strategy of the business is no longer suitable for the business conditions. For example, competitors may have entered the market, technological change may have changed the competitive landscape or there may have been legal changes such as protectionist measures introduced. If the external environment has changed but the strategy has not it means the strategy has drifted from where it needs to be. Managers will need to change their strategy to match the needs of the environment or they will fall further behind.

Progress questions

27 What is meant by strategic drift?

28 Why do you think strategic drift occurs?

29 How do you think a business might avoid strategic drift?

Exam-style questions

Explanation and analysis

1 Explain one factor that would make a "consult" style of leadership appropriate. (4 marks)

2 Explain one way managers of an airline might benefit from contingency planning. (4 marks)

3 A business operates in 20 countries. Explain two ways the culture may vary between the countries it operates in. (6 marks)

4 Analyse how the use of network analysis can help a business to have a shorter payback when developing new products. (9 marks)

5 Analyse the problems a new Chief Executive might face trying to change the culture of a business. (9 marks)

Evaluation

6 A business is experiencing falling profits. Do you think it should replace the Chief Executive? Assess the case for and against and make a judgement. (12 marks)

7 Your business is a multinational with several distinct product categories. Should you adopt a functional or matrix structure? Assess the arguments for and against and make a judgement. (12 marks)

Glossary

A

Ansoff matrix: outlines strategic options in terms of the products offered by a business and the markets it targets.

The **average rate of return** method of investment appraisal calculates the average annual profit as a percentage of the initial investment.

B

Barriers to entry: these make it difficult or expensive for new businesses to enter a market. They include patents, customer/brand loyalty, high start-up costs and limited access to distribution channels.

Benchmarking: when managers identify an aspect of their business that they want to improve and then find another organisation that they can learn from.

C

Capital employed: the total value of all share capital and retained profits and loans of a business.

A **competitive advantage** is when a business can offer better value for money than its rivals.

Consequences of change: are what happens as a result of change.

Corporate Social Responsibility (CSR): a set of policies that demonstrate how committed a business is to the welfare of society by taking responsibility for how their decisions impact on all stakeholders.

Corruption: occurs when people with authority misuse their power.

Current assets: are items that provide a benefit to the business within 12 months.

Current liabilities: represent the money that a business owes and must pay within the next 12 months.

Current ratio: the relationship between current assets and current liabilities.

D

Diseconomies of scale: when the unit costs increase with more output.

Disruptive change: completely changes an industry and the way business is done.

Diversification: where a business sells new products to new customers.

Dividend per share: the rate of return that a holder of ordinary shares receives for each share held.

Dividend yield: measures the dividend per share as a percentage of the share price.

The **driving forces** are those factors in a given situation that make change more likely. They are factors that are pushing for a change in the present situation.

E

Economies of scale: when unit costs decrease with more output.

Efficiency ratios: measure how efficiently resources are used in the business.

Experience curve: shows how unit costs fall as managers become more experienced at what they do over time.

External growth: is where a business joins with another business through merger or takeover.

F

Franchising: is when one business sells the rights to produce or sell its products to another business.

Free trade: occurs when there is no protectionism.

G

Gearing ratio: measures the percentage of the capital of a company that is from fixed interest-bearing sources.

Gross profit margin: the relationship between the gross profit and the sales revenue of a business.

H

High gearing: a high proportion of the capital employed is borrowed.

I

An **income (or profit and loss) statement** is a document that gives the revenues (i.e. income) and costs for a business and the resulting profit or loss for a stated time period.

Incremental change: is change that happens slowly and in small steps.

The **industry environment** describes the conditions of the industry that a business is operating in.

Innovation: occurs when a business develops a new idea and develops it successfully.

Intellectual property: is intangible property that comes from creativity.

An **interest rate** is the cost of borrowing money and the reward paid to savers.

Internal growth or "organic" growth: is where a business expands its operations using its own resources or by enhancing sales internally.

Intrapreneurship: when a business encourages people within the business to be more entrepreneurial.

Inventory turnover: measures how often inventory is replaced in a year.

Investment appraisal: is where managers assess different projects to decide which ones to invest in.

Investment decisions: involve a business spending money on a project now with the aim of generating returns in the future.

J

Joint ventures: where two or more businesses agree to cooperate in a particular area of business.

K

Kaizen: is a Japanese word for "continuous improvement".

L

A **leader** is someone who gives orders and is followed by others.

Liquidity: measures the ability of a business to pay its current liabilities.

Low gearing: a low proportion of the capital employed is borrowed.

M

Market development: where a business sells its existing products in new markets.

Market penetration: where a business sells more of its existing products to its existing customers.

Mechanistic organisations: have clearly defined roles and procedures.

A **mission** sets out why a business exists.

A **multinational** is a business that has bases in more than one country.

N

Net migration: is the difference between the number of immigrants (people coming into a region) and the number of emigrants (people leaving a region) throughout the year.

Net present value: equals present value (today's value of future cash inflows and outflows) minus the initial cost of the investment.

Network analysis: is a visual representation of the different activities involved in a project, the order they must be carried out in and the time they take.

New product development: where a business sells new products to its existing customers.

O

An **objective** is a quantifiable target.

Offshoring: occurs when a business moves production from its own country overseas.

Organic organisations: are more fluid and have less fixed rules, relationships and procedures.

Organisational (or corporate) culture: refers to the attitudes and values of employees.

Overtrading: occurs when a business grows too fast and encounters liquidity problems.

P

Payable days: measures how much is owed by the business in terms of days of sales.

The **payback** method of investment appraisal calculates the time in years and months it would take to repay the initial cost of the investment.

The **payback period** measures how long it takes to repay the initial cost of the investment.

Porter's Five Forces Analysis: sets out five external influences that determine the intensity of the competition in a market and the likely impact on profitability.

Pressures for change: are factors that are making change happen.

Price/earnings ratio: shows the relationship between the earnings per share and the market price of the share.

Process innovation: develops new ways of doing things.

Product innovation: develops new products successfully.

Profit: measures the difference between revenue and costs.

A **profit centre** is a part of the business for which revenues and costs and profits are measured.

Profit margin: measures the profit as a percentage of the sales.

Profitability ratios: a means of measuring different types of profit in relation to sales revenue or capital employed.

Protectionism: occurs when a country introduces measures to protect its own producers against foreign competition.

R

Ratio: one thing measured in terms of another.

Receivables days: measures how much is owed to the business in terms of days of sales.

Research and development: involves scientific research to develop new products and processes.

Resisting forces: create a pressure to keep things as they are and not change.

Retrenchment: is when a business reduces in size.

Return on capital employed: measures profit relative to the capital employed as a percentage.

S

Stakeholder: an individual or group who has an interest in a business. They can be affected by a business decision and/or have their views considered as part of the decision.

A **stakeholder map** categorises stakeholders in terms of their level of interest and their level of power.

A **statement of financial position** the financial document that lists all the assets and liabilities of a business on a specified date.

A **strategy** is a long-term plan of action to achieve an objective.

Strategic drift: occurs when the current strategy of the business is no longer suitable for the business conditions.

Strategic positioning: describes how a business competes relative to other businesses within a chosen market with chosen products.

SWOT analysis: an examination of the strengths and weaknesses (internal) a business has and the opportunities and threats (external) it faces.

Synergy: when bringing two businesses together leads to an organisation that is more successful with the elements combined than it was when they were separate.

T

Triple Bottom Line: measure of the performance of a business in terms of Profit, People and Planet.

U

Urbanisation: occurs when people move to the city from the countryside.

W

Window dressing: changes made in the accounts of a business in order to present a more favourable picture to the users of the accounts, e.g. assets such as "goodwill" are overstated to make the business look better than it is.

Answers

Chapter 1 – case studies, progress questions, exam-style questions

Case studies

Johnson and Johnson

1 Two factors that influence the mission of Johnson and Johnson are:
- What the founders want because people will try and follow the founders' wishes.
- What investors want because they are the owners and so employees will want to please them.
- What the general views of society are because this influences what is regarded as acceptable and what is expected of businesses.

Any two of the above would be valid.

2 The potential benefits to Johnson and Johnson of producing a mission statement include:
- It clarifies for all stakeholders what the business cares about, why it exists and its priorities; this provides a focus.
- It helps employees understand what they are there to do, what is expected of them and how to behave in a given situation so they have greater clarity.
- It can lead to greater alignment, better coordination of decisions and a better sense for everyone of why they are doing what they do; this can lead to more efficiency.

Progress questions

1 The possible stakeholders of a school are the staff, the students and the parents.

2 This statement is false; shareholders are stakeholders but many stakeholders are not shareholders, e.g. suppliers and distributors.

3 One way in that stakeholder mapping may be useful is that it can identify the relative power and interest of different groups and can decide how to deal with the different groups. For example, you may want to keep some groups well informed, but for others they may need less regular contact. This means managers know how best to use their resources and target them effectively to the right stakeholder groups.

4 This statement is false; it is the plan to achieve the objectives.

5 SWOT analysis is an analysis of the strengths, weaknesses, opportunities and threats facing a business.

6 Three stakeholders in a business can be chosen from: employees, investors, suppliers, the community, the government, customers.

7 The axes used on a stakeholder map are: the levels of interest and power.

8 Two possible objectives of a business can be chosen from: profits, survival, cash flow, growth.

Exam-style questions

Explanation and analysis

1 One benefit to a large business of having a clear objective is that it helps unify employees to know what they are doing and why. This means it can help clarify what to do in any situation because they have specific target with time limit. This leads to more efficient and more focused decision making; this should lead to better more profitable decisions.

2 One benefit of stakeholder mapping when changing strategy is that it can identify which stakeholder groups have the most interest and power. This means that the managers can work most closely with these, e.g. involve them most in the change process; they can therefore use their resources and time efficiently. They can decide which groups need to be kept regularly informed and which can have less time spent on them (e.g. if low interest and low power). This ensures an efficient use of management time.

3 Two ways a stakeholder groups might be affected by a decision to invest in new technology include:
- It may lead to job losses or a need for retraining because fewer people are needed due to the technology. This affects employees' morale and may affect the ability of the business to recruit and keep staff.
- It may lead to better-quality products at a lower price due to the technology. This affects customers and may affect sales and in the long term the profits and rewards to another stakeholder group: the investors.

4 A focus on short termism might affect two of the functional areas of a business. It may lead to:
- Less investment in training because the managers do not want to train people for the long term. This affects the human resources function.
- Less investment in research and development because managers will not be considering developing new products for the long term. This will affect the operations function.

5 SWOT analysis can help a business to change strategy effectively because it:
- Can identify strengths of the business. A new strategy may build on this strength; for example, if a business is strong at entering new markets then a new strategy may look for more market opportunities.
- Can identify weaknesses. A new strategy may be developed to protect against weaknesses; for example, if a business has a lack of new products in the pipeline then a strategy may focus on research and development and investing to broaden the portfolio.
- Can identify opportunities. A new strategy may be developed to exploit the opportunities. For example, if the move is towards more online shopping a retailer may look to move its sales online.
- Can identify threats and may develop strategy to protect against these. For example, if a threat is that taxes in the product will be increased managers may look to cut costs (e.g. through greater efficiencies) to offset higher taxes.

Evaluation

6 Whether or not reviewing the mission statement is a priority may depend on the cause of the poor performance; is it because the business has lost its way and needs to redefine itself? Or is it, for example, because of external factors? The key is to address the cause of the poor performance. Rewriting the mission statement is not likely in itself to improve performance if the problem is to do with the economy, for example. The key is understanding the cause of the problems. It may be that people within the business have lost a sense of what matters. It may be that conditions have changed and the business needs a new way of operating and a new direction. In this case a new mission statement may be helpful to rethink and look again at what the business is, what it values and what it wants to be. Reviewing the mission may also be a good way to listen to different views and get everyone in agreement about the direction of the business.

Whether reviewing the mission is a priority therefore depends on the underlying cause of poor performance and whether coming together to discuss the purpose of the business will help to improve this.

7 Involving stakeholders in a change of strategy may help overcome some opposition and help to make sure it is successful. Involving the stakeholders (i.e. those affected by the business activity) may help provide some useful insights and generate useful cooperation. This can lead to better decisions being made with more ideas involved and people working more effectively together.

However, managers may not like what they hear when they involve people; it may be that there are a lot of ideas but they are not very good. This may depend on how well informed the stakeholders are. Each stakeholder may be protecting his or her own interests whereas managers should be protecting the long-term interests of the business and its owners. The value of involving stakeholders may also depend on which stakeholder group is involved; it may be important to pay attention to and involve some more than others (e.g. those with a high level of interest and power). It may be possible to ignore those with little power and interest but some groups you cannot easily avoid. Whether to involve stakeholders may therefore depend on their power and their level of interest. It will also depend on what value they can add with their ideas and the time managers have; if they are short of time they may not have the time to consult.

Chapter 2 – progress questions, exam-style questions

Progress questions

1 It is necessary to examine the balance sheet and the profit and loss statement of a business because they provide different pieces of information. A balance sheet shows the value of assets at a particular moment in time; the profit and loss shows the income and profits

generated over the last year. We need both for a good picture of what has happened; for example a balance sheet may show a high level of assets but we need to see the profit and loss (income statement) to see the performance in the year before and whether last year the business was actually profitable (it might not have been!). Similarly a business may be profitable but we need the balance sheet to see what its total assets are.

2   Three stakeholder groups that might be interested in the financial performance of a particular business are suppliers, investors and rivals.

3   It is important to look at profitability and not just profit because there is a need to place the profit figure in context; for example, managers may want to compare profits relative to sales or capital employed.

4   A business can have a low operating profit margin but a high return on capital employed if its sales are high. With high sales the profit per sale may be low but this will add up to a high profit overall relative to the capital employed.

5   The current assets of a business are $12 million. The current liabilities are $8 million.
    Current ratio = current assets/current liabilities = 12/8 = 1.5

6   A business may not want too high a current ratio because there could be too much inventory (which could be stolen or lose value) or too much money in cash which is not earning a return. The business would be liquid but the money may be sitting idle in assets when it could be used to earn a higher return elsewhere.

7   A business will not want its current ratio to be too low because this may mean it has problems paying its current liabilities; there could be liquidity problems.

8   The capital employed of a business is $40 million and the long-term borrowing is $5 million.
    Gearing = long-term liability/capital employed = (5/40) × 100 = 12.5%
    If the business borrowed an additional $3 million:
    Gearing = (8/43) × 100 = 18.6%

9   A business may not want its gearing ratio to be too high because it may be risky as the business will have to repay interest. Even if profits are zero the business will need to pay the interest; this can create problems and is a risk.

10 A business may not want its gearing ratio to be too low because it may mean it is not borrowing sufficiently and missing investment opportunities which could earn high returns. By not borrowing, a business may miss an investment with a very high return.

11 A business may not want its inventory turnover to be too low because it may mean inventory is not selling; this could be because the business is stocking products that do not appeal. This means the business may be left with unsold inventory which it has to throw away or discount to eventually sell it. This means a loss of profit.

12 One reason why the P/E ratio of a company may be high is because there is a high demand for the shares, which pulls up the price. For example, investors may be optimistic about the leader's strategy or the likely success of a new product just launched.

13 A business benefits from introducing profit centres because it may make employees more aware of performance; they will be able to see what the profits of their profit centre are (e.g. their division or store). Being able to know the profits may motivate the staff; it may enable them to measure performance more clearly and monitor their progress against targets.

14 A business may benefit from analysing the performance of its profit centres because it can identify how different parts of business perform; it can analyse any differences and adopt best practice and manage poor practices. By analysing profit centres the business may identify parts of the business to grow more and other parts to sell off.

15 Profit margin is profit as a percentage of sales whereas the return on capital employed is profit as a percentage of the capital employed. It is possible to have a low profit margin but high return on capital employed provided enough is sold.

16 Shareholder ratios include: P/E ratio; dividend per share; dividend yield.

17 Efficiency ratios include: inventory ratio; receivable days; payable days.

18 A profit centre is part of the business for which revenues and costs are measured.

19 The Triple Bottom Line measures the performance of a business in terms of Profit, People and Planet.

Exam-style questions

Explanation and analysis

1   A low current ratio may signal liquidity problems because it means that the current assets are less than current liabilities.

2   A potential supplier might consider the inventory turnover ratio to see how often inventories are replaced, and payable days which will give an idea of how long it takes for the business to be paid.

3   A potential investor might consider the P/E ratio as this shows the price relative to profits and so is an indication of whether the share price is low or high. The investor may also look at the dividend yield as this shows the dividends as a percentage of the share price and so show if the return is good. An investor might also look at the return on capital employed to get a sense of how profitable the business was and therefore what might happen in terms of the share price and dividends.

4   A high gearing ratio means the borrowing of the business will be relatively high. This means it may be difficult to repay interest payments if profits are low; interest repayments will not vary with the profitability of the business, so there is a risk. Managers may therefore not want gearing to be too high because of this risk.

5   Introducing profit centres may enable managers to compare the performance of different shops within the overall chain. Managers may identify differences in costs or revenues that can be analysed and managers can learn from this analysis. They may be able to learn from differences and make changes in different stores to increase revenue or reduce costs. Having profit centres may mean that the managers of the different stores may be competitive and try to improve their performance relative to other stores. This competition may be good for the profits of the business as a whole.

Evaluation

6   Financial ratio analysis may provide insight into areas such as liquidity, efficiency and profitability. The use of ratios may highlight risks such as low liquidity and high gearing. This will help you to take a view about the likely share price and ability to pay out dividends. If gearing is high and liquidity is poor, for example, this may mean that the share price is unlikely to rise until such problems are dealt with.

    However, using this particular data is backward looking – it refers to last year not the future and so shows what has happened whereas investors will be interested in what is going to happen. This data may also have been window dressed to look favourable; for example, the value for the inventories may not reflect what could actually be achieved if the inventory was sold today. Also financial ratios may be useful but they do not show the whole picture, e.g. the future strategy of the business and external conditions the business will face, its environmental impact, the quality of leadership or the morale of staff. Ideally an investor would have an overall picture of where the business is headed and this would help put the ratios in context. Profitability may be low now, but if the strategy is good it may be expected to rise.

    Overall financial analysis is useful but care needs to be taken when assuming the future will be like the past, and investors may want a broader range of measures to make a better decision.

7   Liquidity is essential for the business to survive. A business needs to be able to pay its bills or it may not continue trading. Typically managers consider the current ratio (current assets:current liabilities) and look for a ratio of between 1.5 to 1 or 2 to 1. This shows that the current assets cover the current liabilities. However, profitability is a typical measure of whether it is worth being in business; if financial returns are the objective and managers cannot generate sufficient profitability in the desired timeframe then the resources for the business may be better used elsewhere. So both ratios are important: the aim of many businesses is to be profitable so this is the key long term, but to survive liquidity is needed. Without liquidity the business may not survive because it cannot pay its bills; without profitability there may be no point surviving.

Chapter 3 – case studies, progress questions, exam-style questions

Case studies

Ofo

1   Ofo is struggling to make a profit because:
    - There are several competitors so rivalry is high which makes the market price competitive and tends to push down prices and profits.
    - Customers have choice and so there is high buyer power; this allows the buyers to push down prices because the businesses need their orders. The lower prices push down profits.
    - There are alternative ways of getting around the city so the substitute threat is high. This pushes prices down and reduces profits.
    - Entering the market is not that difficult so the entry threat is high. This again pushes prices down because if profits were too high, other businesses would enter and bring down prices.

2   There may be a reduction in number of providers due to a fall in the overall profits available because of higher than expected repair and maintenance costs. With lower than expected profits there is

less incentive to compete in the industry. On the other hand the convenience of renting rather than owning a bicycle is likely to continue as part of an overall trend towards rental, assuming the fees are appropriate and bicycles reliable. Better technology, making it easier to locate and track bikes, will make them more appealing and development in technology may reduce some of the repair costs.

However, the appeal of the market will depend on how well managed the process can be. Better management of bicycles is needed so that there are fewer abandoned bikes and less mess around the city with bikes left everywhere which authorities may object to. It is unlikely that rentals will stop but the nature of the service may evolve.

Sonos

1 With reference to Porter's five forces, in this industry:
   - There is increasing competition in the industry which increases rivalry because more businesses are competing for business.
   - There are many potential suppliers of components meaning that the supplier power is likely to be low.

2 Whether Sonos should cut prices may depend on:
   - How sensitive demand is to price. If price is very sensitive this means that a price cut will lead to a bigger percentage of the sales and revenue will rise.
   - Whether the business thinks this will start a price war. This will reduce profit margins and may damage the brand image and so a business may be reluctant to start this.
   - Overall impact on profit margins and return on capital employed.
   - Whether through further innovation it can justify existing or even higher prices for new models.
   - Desired positioning in the market. By lowering prices the business may reduce the perceived value of the brand.

Progress questions

1 Increased barriers to entry may enable existing businesses to earn higher profits; this will encourage more businesses to want to enter, which would mean profits are shared amongst more firms, but with barriers to entry they will not be able to enter.

2 With more substitutes customers will switch away to cheaper alternatives; existing businesses will not be able to push up prices as much due to availability of substitutes. This means profits in the industry are likely to be lower.

3 Greater supplier power means the suppliers can push up prices because the buyers will not have the ability to switch away; this may be because of the specialist skill of the supplier or the control over some technology. These increases in the suppliers' prices increase the costs of business and reduce the profits.

4 A manager might try to increase barriers to entry by getting the government to introduce barriers such as protectionist measures. This limits the number of foreign products coming into a country or increases their prices through additional taxes. Managers might also try to develop more brand loyalty so customers are less likely to switch away to new entrants. Through branding and advertising, managers may try to develop loyalty to the brand. Finally, they might try to gain control of supplies to make it more difficult to enter.

5 A manager might try to reduce rivalry in an industry through mergers and takeovers. By joining with or taking over another business this removes a competitor and means the new bigger business has a larger market share and less rivalry.

6 Greater buyer power in an industry might reduce profits of the businesses competing in an industry. Powerful buyers can push down prices because the businesses supplying them rely on their business and this can reduce profits in an industry.

7 An entry threat refers to the likelihood that another business will enter the market, e.g. does it have the funds or expertise to enter?

8 Rivalry occurs when businesses compete with the same products for customers; substitute threat occurs when a customer switches between businesses that provide a similar benefit but in a different way. For example, a taxi and a bus both transport you but differently.

9 Buyer power is the influence that buyers have on a business. If your business relies on one buyer that buyer has significant power. A buyer with strong power can push prices down.

10 Supplier power is the influence that suppliers have over the price they set; the more power they have the more they can charge. Suppliers will have power if their buyers do not have many alternative sources of supply.

11 A business may change one of the five forces by:
   - Taking over a rival to reduce rivalry.
   - Taking over a supplier to reduce supplier power because you now own the supplier.
   - Developing brand loyalty to reduce buyer power by making buyers prefer its product to others.

Exam-style questions

Explanation and analysis

1 An increase in buyer power may reduce profits as buyers have the power to push prices down – they can force suppliers to accept the lower prices to keep the orders.

2 A business might reduce the power of suppliers in its industry by merging or taking over the suppliers; this means the business can then set supplier prices because they own the supplier.

3 Two ways a business might reduce the threat of entry into the industry are:
   - Getting government protection – for example quotas placed on foreign goods – to prevent or limit competition.
   - Getting patent protection for an invention; this prevents the technology being copied.
   - By merging with another business to get a cost advantage through economies of scale; this might make it difficult for others to enter as they will not be able to match the low prices.

4 A greater substitute threat might reduce the profits in an industry. This is because it means customers have more alternatives and therefore can switch away quite easily. A business will have to be price competitive in this situation and cannot easily push prices up. With more options, customers have more power and can leave if the prices are too high. Profits are therefore likely to fall.

5 Less rivalry in an industry may increase profits. This is because with less rivalry the existing businesses have more power in the market because their customers have less choice. Businesses can push up prices and make more profits without fear of price cutting by rivals.

Evaluation

6 The five forces in Porter's model have an impact on profits, e.g. high buyer power, high supplier power, high substitute threat and rivalry are all likely to reduce profits This is because selling prices will be pushed down by buyers, customers can easily switch away if prices are too high and suppliers will push up prices.

However, these forces are not fixed; they can change over time. Managers can also try to influence these forces, e.g. by merging to reduce rivalry, by investing heavily in marketing to create a barrier to entry, by vertical integration to gain more power over suppliers. If a particular force is unfavourable a manager could put together a strategy to try to alter this force and make it work in favour of the business. Therefore managers do not need to accept forces; they can try and influence them. However, this does not mean they can control them.

But the success of this is not totally under their control. For example, the actions of competitors in terms of developing products can influence the substitute threat or the degree of rivalry. Managers do not have to accept the five forces; however, they are not totally under their control.

7 The internet may affect:
   - Buyer power by giving buyers more choice and therefore making an industry less favourable for businesses in that industry.
   - The substitute threat by creating new ways of meeting needs, e.g. direct bookings of people's homes (AirBnB) rather than hotels, or people using Uber rather than taxis. The greater substitute threat makes an industry less favourable for those already in it.
   - Supplier power by reducing it as businesses can find more suppliers more easily; this is favourable for these businesses as it means suppliers have less power.

The internet may therefore give more advantages to customers as buyers, which may reduce profits; however, businesses themselves are buyers and so this may reduce their costs and increase profits. The internet has also created many markets that did not exist before and which offer the opportunities for profits that did not exist before, and this can create favourable opportunities. The answer therefore depends on which force, which business and which market.

Chapter 4 – case studies, progress questions, exam-style questions

Case studies

Johnson & Johnson

1 One reason why laws are necessary to protect consumers is because businesses may try to mislead customers to sell more, or not care about the information or their customers' safety as managers will be so focused on profits. Laws may be needed to control business behaviour.

2 Laws may make it more difficult to make a profit because they may limit the behaviour of businesses. They may limit what a business can sell, e.g. they may not allow guns to be sold. Laws may also limit

how businesses promote products and to whom, e.g. there are often restrictions on the sale of cigarettes. Laws may also prevent businesses from selling in certain markets; for example, a dispute between governments may prevent a business selling in certain countries. However, laws can help businesses to make profits. Laws can open up markets; for example, trade agreements can encourage free trade and access to customers overseas. Laws can also protect a business from other businesses by, for example, limiting monopoly power or unfair competition.

Overall the impact of the law depends on which law is being considered; some may help profits but some may not.

Progress questions

1   One way an employment law might affect a business is that it imposes costs on the business to meet its obligations, e.g. for meeting health and safety regulations.

2   One way competition law might affect a business is by limiting the monopoly power of a business; for example, the growth of the business may be limited.

3   One way an environmental law might affect a business is by limiting how it produces. For example, laws may ensure certain processes are put in place to restrict emissions.

4   One way in which political instability might affect a business is that it may limit investment. Managers may be unwilling to commit to new projects until they have a better sense of what the political environment will be.

5   One way in which corruption can affect a business is that it makes managers reluctant to invest in a country because their ability to succeed may depend on factors outside of their control; competition may not be fair and the environment may be uncertain depending on who is in favour at any moment.

Exam-style questions

Explanation and analysis

1   The law can affect the profits of a business by increasing costs; for example, managers may have to recognise certain employee rights and pay to ensure the working environment is safe and secure. Higher costs would reduce profits.

2   Political instability may lead to less business investment. Managers may be less sure of their future returns and therefore unwilling to commit resources into an investment project because the risk is too high.

3   Giving employees more rights might lead to more people being willing to work because they know, for example, that they cannot be dismissed without a reason and/or that they will get some pay if ill. This could increase the pool of labour that a business can choose from. At the same time, employment rights can increase costs. A business may have to pay redundancy payments or pay for paternity or maternity leave, which adds costs and reduces profits.

4   Corruption in an economy might make it more difficult to do business. There is a lack of transparency and fairness and it may not be clear why one business wins a contract or gets the right to operate and another doesn't. This may make managers reluctant to invest in that country because there is so much uncertainty. Investment may fall, there may be fewer jobs and this may create less work for other businesses who would have been suppliers.

5   The government might want to help entrepreneurs to start up in business because this will encourage business activity. More businesses mean more products and more innovation. This means new goods and services for customers. Businesses also create jobs – jobs within the business itself and with their suppliers. This contributes to economic growth and can help a government's citizens prosper.

Evaluation

6   The bribe may enable you to win the contract and earn profits. This may help your business and your career. You may argue that others are also bribing and therefore you are only doing what others are doing and in some sense this is making it "fairer" (if illegal).

However, you might argue that this is illegal behaviour and therefore you should not be doing it. It leaves you open to prosecution; this could lead to you being imprisoned and your could be business open to prosecution as well.

Your willingness to bribe may depend on the size of the contract and the gains from this; the bigger the rewards the more tempting it may be. Overall, bribery is immoral and illegal. It puts you and your business at risk.

7   Changes in the law could increase your costs. In a hotel the law may impose extra regulations such as new health and safety regulations; this may mean new equipment has to be installed, changes may be needed to the premises and additional processes instated, all of which may increase costs and reduce profits. Laws may also affect marketing – for example, it may be made difficult to promote to people who have visited the website unless they have given their permission.

However, laws may prevent competitors from falsely advertising or from cheating in some way to win customers (e.g. spreading false rumours about competitors). This can help the hotel to make more revenue and increase profits.

Changes in the law can reduce profits, therefore, but it is not true to say they will always reduce profits.

Chapter 5 – case studies, progress questions, exam-style questions

Case studies

GDP

1   The world's national income has typically increased by around 3.5% a year.

2   These changes in world GDP might increase demand generally for goods and services. With more income people have more purchasing power and have the ability to spend and buy more. The impact will be greater for income elastic products because demand is sensitive to income changes; demand for inferior products will fall because they have a negative income elasticity of demand which means that with more income demand falls.

3   GDP is likely to be a significant influence on demand for some products. This is because income is a determinant of purchasing power. With more income people are likely to spend more, and with less income they will spend less. The greater the income elasticity of demand the greater the effect of any change in income; if demand is income inelastic then the impact of a change in income will be smaller.

However, there are other factors that influence the success of a business, e.g. the marketing mix and competitor actions. If the pricing strategy is wrong, for example, this will put off customers and reduce demand. If competitors launch a better value product this will take sales way from the business.

Success is also affected by costs, e.g. of labour, energy and other resources. If these costs increase this may damage profits and financial success.

Income may have some impact here (e.g. increased demand for labour may bid up wages generally) but there are other factors such as import costs due to exchange rate changes so the changes in costs are often not linked to income.

Ultimately the success of business may depend on the strategy developed by management; are managers looking ahead and can they develop an appropriate strategy for the circumstances? Income is one factor, particularly for demand, that managers need to plan for, but it is one of many.

Malaysian Ringitt

1   **a)** Around 3.5 Malaysian Ringitts equals US$1 in 2009 **b)** around 4.5 Ringitts in 2017.

2   The effect of the changes in the exchange rate between 2009 and 2017 are that buying dollars is more expensive to Malaysian importers. This means it will be more expensive to buy imports from the US which will affect any Malaysian company that relies on US imported inputs or that tries to sell on US products.

For Malaysian exporters US buyers will find the dollar buys more Ringitts and therefore Malaysian products will be cheaper in dollars. This can help stimulate demand for Malaysian products in the US.

Cobalt mining

1   The price of cobalt will be influenced by demand. Demand is increasing at the moment and this is pushing up prices given the available supply. Demand is increasing because of the demand for lithium batteries and the growth in demand for electric cars. Over time more resources will be put into the supply of cobalt and this may bring the price down (depending on how much demand continues to grow). If demand is growing more than supply, prices will tend to rise. If supply is rising more than demand, prices will tend to fall.

Progress questions

1   Products that might have demand that is sensitive to income include: luxury holidays; private healthcare; luxury cars.

2   Products that might have demand that is not very sensitive to income include: salt; milk; shoelaces; pencils.

3   Demand for some supermarket own-brand items may fall as customers switch to branded products. Demand for bicycles may fall as people trade up to mopeds and cars.

4   The removal of protectionist measures might affect local businesses because:

- It may open up new markets allowing more exports and sales. This may help demand and boost sales.

- It may open up new suppliers and enable access to new cheaper, better-quality supplies. This may reduce the costs of local businesses and help profits.

5   Higher interest rates make borrowing more expensive. This deters borrowing and so is likely to reduce demand for houses (especially because money is usually borrowed to buy houses). High borrowing costs, therefore, are likely to lead to less borrowing and less demand for houses. This is likely to affect sales and profits of housebuilders. Housebuilders may need to find ways of reducing costs to bring prices down and/or build different types of cheaper housing.

6   The price of land will depend on demand and supply for this resource. Supply may be affected by restrictions on what land can be used for and what can be built there. Demand will be affected by incomes and the cost of borrowing.

7   The price of oil might fall if there is less demand, e.g. due to slower growth in the economy leading to less demand for energy or due to cheaper alternative sources of energy, meaning customers change from oil to other products. Another reason could be due to more supply, e.g. new oil reserves discovered with new technology. Greater supply means that at the old price there would be a surplus, which will lead prices to fall.

8   A chain of coffee shops might respond to an increase in the price of coffee by:
- Passing on increased costs to customers via higher prices. The ability and willingness of a business to push up prices will depend on the price elasticity of demand.
- Looking for ways of savings costs to offset this.

9   Inflation occurs when there is a sustained rise in the general price level. Deflation occurs when there is a sustained fall in the general price level.

10 GDP stands for Gross Domestic Product; this measures the national income of a country over a given period of time – usually a year.

11 Lower interest rates might:
- Reduce the cost of borrowing, leading to more profits.
- Encourage borrowing and more investment, helping the business prepare for the future.
- Make it cheaper for customers to borrow, leading to higher demand because they have access to more funds.

12 The price of oil will be affected by the demand for oil and the supply of oil. With more demand the price is likely to increase; with more supply the price is likely to fall.

13 The infrastructure of an economy includes transportation, communication systems, energy supplies and telecommunications.

Exam-style questions

Explanation and analysis

1   A good-quality infrastructure might make it cheaper and quicker to transport products around, allowing more sales. This may be because of a better road or rail system. With more sales there is more revenue and profits.

2   One way in which globalisation might affect a business is by allowing more access to more markets, increasing potential demand. For example, there may be less protectionism, allowing more free trade and sales overseas.

3   An increase in the value of a country's currency means it is more expensive in terms of other currencies. This may lead to less demand for many products exported. This is because products will be more expensive in the foreign currency. This will lead to a fall in sales. The effect will be greater the more price elastic demand is. The exporter may also benefit from lower import costs if any of the components are imported; this is because the stronger currency means that less is needed for the same amount of foreign currency.

4   Higher unemployment means that less people are in work. This reduces their incomes and means they have less spending power. This will lead to less demand for more products. The effect will be higher with income elastic products which are more sensitive to income changes. With less demand profits may fall unless a business can reduce costs.

5   More free trade may mean easier access to markets because there is less protectionism (e.g. no tariffs or quotas). This should create more potential demand and sales, boosting profits. It may also bring in more competitors from abroad, reducing demand and profits.

Evaluation

6   If the government gives protectionist support then this may help to protect against cheap foreign competition, protecting demand and sales. This is because the number of foreign goods sold in a country would be limited (e.g. with a quota) or be more expensive (e.g. with a tariff). This should boost sales of domestic products.

However, introducing protectionist measures may lead to retaliation from foreign governments. This may then reduce your access to markets to sell to and to access supplies.

Overall the effect may depend on how much protectionism is introduced and the impact of this on domestic sales, and whether there is any retaliation.

7   An increase in the value of a currency is likely to reduce exports as exports will be more expensive in foreign currency and all other factors remain constant; the effect will depend on price elasticity of demand for the product. This means sales, revenue and profits may fall. Also, buying in products from abroad will be cheaper in domestic currency; this means direct foreign competition will be cheaper, which could reduce your sales and profits. However, buying in materials and supplies could be cheaper, which could increase profits.

Ultimately, the effect depends on how much the exchange rate changes and against which currencies; how much the business exports, how much it buys in imported materials and how much it competes directly in domestic markets against foreign competition. Your shareholders are your owners and so you probably should tell them – they will discover eventually and it may be better to warn them in advance. However, it is best to do so with a clear idea of the impact so they can make an informed judgement about what to do next.

Chapter 6 – case studies, progress questions, exam-style questions

Case studies

Population changes

1   The growing population in China and India could increase demand especially for some products (e.g. healthcare); this is because there are more potential customers to buy these products; if the population is ageing this will affect certain products bought by older people. Population growth will also increase the working population, depending on the age breakdown and the ages at which people start and finish work. A greater workforce could make labour cheaper as businesses have more people to choose from.

Japan's ageing population

1   Whether an ageing population creates more opportunities than threats for business will depend on the business and how it responds. For example, an ageing population is likely to increase demand for healthcare products and for care homes; it is less likely to increase demand for late-night bars and mopeds. However, the effect does depend on how the business responds; for example, managers of schools can offer classes for the elderly, and managers of health clubs can focus on fitness for the elderly, provided the managers see the opportunities early enough and take the appropriate actions.

In general, an ageing population places more demands on the health and benefits system and may be associated with fewer people working and paying tax. This can be difficult for government finances and lead to more taxes generally for businesses as well as individuals. This may reduce the income individuals have or the profits businesses have, and this may reduce demand for goods and services.

The overall effect of an ageing population will depend on whether it is foreseen and planned for, e.g. not all populations are ageing so managers could start to target other markets for sales and recruitment if they were worried that it would badly affect sales in existing countries. Populations do not age suddenly so managers should have time to plan ahead in terms of where they compete and how they compete.

Danone

1   Focusing on stakeholder needs may be the right thing to do. Regardless of the financial impact, the managers may want to do it because they believe in it. It may benefit society, with staff being better treated, with suppliers being treated fairly and with the community gaining from investment. Managers may want Danone to be a good corporate citizen. However, the managers were appointed by shareholders who are the owners, and ultimately – it may be argued – Danone needs to meet their needs first. Some argue that it is not up to managers to try and meet stakeholder needs; they should make profits for shareholders, and give this profit to the shareholders who can then decide individually what they want to do with it. It is not for managers – some would say – to allocate funds and make decisions in the interests of stakeholders.

However, it is possible to argue that looking after stakeholders benefits shareholders. Working well with employees may help motivation and lead to more productivity, more ideas and more cooperation. Working well with suppliers may lead to better-quality supplies, more reliable deliveries and preferential treatment. So working with stakeholders may actually help the company's profits and reputation and this can benefit shareholders as well.

Samsung

1   Samsung's decision to spend more money on research and development might benefit its stakeholders by creating jobs for employees because the company will need people to do this work. It may also create orders for suppliers which will help the employees keep jobs and help Samsung's profits. Another group that might benefit is the customers because they might get new and better products as a result of the innovation.

2   Businesses may want to make decisions on the basis of how it helps society because they feel it is the right thing to do. They may also think it helps the business financially. This is because it may appeal more to customers, employees and investors. This may lead to a wider pool of employees, more customers and more potential investors. It may also prevent bad publicity because the business is seen to do the right thing; this may avoid negative media coverage.

However, some of the gains may be difficult to quantify when assessing an investment, e.g. impact on reputation. Also, some may argue that provided the business is legal it should not try to be socially responsible – that is not the role of business.

Overall it may depend on the mission and objectives of the business – how important is it to the owners and managers to be socially responsible, how important are profits? The values of the owners and managers will drive what is considered when assessing an investment.

China's digital economy

1   Digital developments can benefit businesses in China by enabling better communications (e.g. through mobile or online technology). This can make it cheaper and easier to manage and grow a business. It may provide more information (e.g. through big data) and lead to better management. Digital technology may also create new markets (such as computer games and streamed music) which provide more opportunities for profits. It also allows the business to grow globally (online) and challenge competitors (e.g. through online banking, challenging existing providers).

Raya

1   The price of imported materials might affect the price at which the business sells. For example, if Raya feels that it can pass any price increases on or if it wants to pass on any price reductions then a change in costs will affect prices. However, if Raya cannot or does not want to change prices in line with the price of imported materials, this will affect its profit margins. For example, higher imported material costs will reduce profits margins, and lower imported material prices will increase profit margins.

2   A change in imported material prices will have an effect on the selling price or profit margins of a business. For example, an increase in costs may lead to a higher price as the costs are passed on or may lead to lower profit margins if they are absorbed. The ability to pass on prices may depend on the price elasticity of demand. For example, an increase in costs may be more likely to be passed on if demand is not very sensitive to price, i.e. it is price inelastic.

However, success will depend on its marketing as a whole, its targeting, its positioning, its strategy, its people and the quality of its operations. Many factors will combine to determine success. For example, a business needs to design products that meet people's needs, and it should promote these effectively. If there are low levels of demand, quality issues and lots of competition then the material costs are just one small part of the success or failure of a business.

Progress questions

1   Greater urbanisation might increase demand for goods and services in this area. It might mean more people in one area so it is easier for marketers to target and access potential customers. Greater urbanisation might also mean greater congestion, transportation and pollution problems and a general strain on the infrastructure. This might affect the ease of doing business and increase costs for business, thus reducing profits.

2   Urbanisation occurs when there is an increase in the movement of people to the cities.

3   Corporate Social Responsibility occurs when a business acts in the interests of society.

4   The shareholder concept means that managers want to meet the needs of shareholders and the focus is on profit. The stakeholder concept focuses on the needs of a wider range of different interests affected by the businesses such as suppliers, customers, the community and employees.

5   Migration occurs when people move from one region to another.

6   Digital technology creates the opportunity to do business in new ways; for example Spotify has challenged the existing music companies by offering streaming and AirBnB has challenged existing holiday companies. This creates the chance to make revenue by doing things differently and making profits.

Exam-style questions

Explanation and analysis

1   An increase in migration into a country influences the labour market because it will mean there are more people there to select from (depending on their age and skills). This might lead to more businesses setting up because the people and skills are there. It might allow business to expand more easily because they can find the staff they need. It might lead to more competitive businesses because they can get better-quality staff.

2   Managers might decide to become more socially responsible because they are more aware of what is right – this may come from greater awareness of issues in society or because of more information and communications. Changes in society's views may mean there is social pressure – pressure from customers, employees and investors – for a business to change if it wants more staff, customers and investors, and it may mean mangers decide this is now the right thing to do.

3   The benefits to a retailer of moving its operations online could be lower costs of operating the business because it may not need to pay for physical stores. This could make it cheaper to set up and more likely to set up because the returns will be higher. Going online may also provide greater access to more markets because it can reach customers globally 24 hours a day every day of the year. Online retailing also makes it easier to track how and when customers buy and what else they look at. This can help a business understand its customers and change what it does to boost profits.

4   Social attitudes to environmental issues might affect a business because it may lead to different ways of producing – for example, a business may have to use local suppliers rather than transporting products all over the world. These suppliers may be more expensive and potentially not as good quality, but they may be more acceptable to customers. Changing social attitudes may also lead to different products being produced – for example more paper bags and less plastic bags – this may help some businesses (if they focus on paper) but not others (if they focus on plastic). Businesses may need to review their processes and products to meet customer wants.

5   A change in the composition of the workforce can affect labour supply. It may affect the number of people available and the skills they have. This can affect the typical wages being paid. It can affect the ease with which businesses recruit, which can affect the ease of expanding and the quality of the work done. This can affect the competitiveness of a business.

Evaluation

6   There are advantages of being online. It may be cheaper than having to build and run stores. It can also enable a business to operate globally because it can access customers online 24 hours a day. However, it does require the technical expertise to run a site properly and it does require the logistical operations to deliver products to and collect returns from customers in different locations. This may be complex and expensive. Whether to go online depends on:

- The nature of the product – some products sell better online than others; for example, people may be willing to buy most clothes online but perhaps would want a personalised service and fitting for a wedding dress.

- Access to and costs of distribution network; a business may have to define certain areas to operate in depending on its ability to distribute door to door or distribute through others' stores.

- The costs of returning goods. The costs of delivering and then collecting if it is not satisfactory may not be cost effective for cheap T shirts for example.

- The savings made on physical outlets.

- Whether it is worth having a mixed offer – e.g. using shops to look at products and get advice and pick up orders.

7   A business may want to buy Fair Trade beans because the managers think this is the right thing to do; they think is it morally right to pay a "fair" price to suppliers and that business is not all about profit. However, this costs more and could decrease profits. Whether to use Fair Trade products therefore depends on:

- The mission, objectives and values of the owners and senior managers; how important is doing the right thing compared to profits?

- The difference in costs; if this is a minor difference the decision may not be so difficult.

- The ethics of customers and willingness to pay more (which determines whether you can pass on higher costs). If customers prefer Fair Trade then actually it may be possible to increase the price and sell more. Profits may actually be higher with Fair Trade and therefore the business wins financially as well as by doing the right thing.

Chapter 7 – case studies, progress questions, exam-style questions

Case studies

GazProm

1 Two factors that might determine the profits made by this project include the future price of gas, because this will determine the expected revenue earnings from an investment project; the higher the price of oil, other things being equal, the higher the profit. The costs of completing and running it are also important. This is a very complex project requiring significant engineering skills. The project may face unexpected technological issues as well as political ones which affect costs and the actual profits compared to the expected ones.

2 The non-financial factors that might have been considered before going ahead with this investment project include the impact on political relations with China and the West. The project is to build relations between Russia and China, and it highlights differences with the West. This project would score significant political points for Russia against the West. It would also bring great prestige to have undertaken and succeeded in such a major project – it is extremely complex and a major engineering feat. This again would be to the Russian government's credit. The technology required may require innovation and new ways of doing things which may have a benefit for other Russian industries in terms of what can be achieved and at what cost.

Progress questions

1 The answer to this will depend on what is happening in your country at the moment and whether it could have been anticipated or not.

2 On the basis of this information alone, Project X, as it pays back quicker, which is the key if liquidity is a concern.

3 Payback = 2 years + 5/15 = 2 years + 1/3 of a year = 2 Years 4 months

Total profit	30
Average profit per year	7.5
ARR	37.5%

4 There is a relatively short payback and a high ARR; it looks like an attractive investment option.

5

Year	Net inflow $m	Discount factor (10%)	Present Value $ = net inflow × discount factor $m
0	−30		
1	10	0.91	9.1
2	15	0.83	12.45
3	15	0.75	11.25
4	20	0.68	13.6

Present value	$46.4 million
Net present value	$16.4 million

6 Which project to choose given this data depends on the business and its priorities. Project A has a shorter payback and this is appealing, but it is less attractive in terms of overall returns. If the business can afford to wait then Project B is more attractive with a 14% return on average per year and a higher net present value.

7 The payback period is the time taken to repay the initial investment.

8 Average rate of return is the average profit as a percentage of initial investment.

9 The net present value is the difference between discounted values of future expected inflows and the initial cost of the project.

10 Risk means the probability of something going wrong and damaging the business.

11 Two examples of non-financial criteria that might influence an investment decision are: ethics; impact on the brand; impact on stakeholders.

Exam-style questions

Explanation and analysis

1 One benefit of the payback method rather than the ARR is that it shows time taken to repay investment. This is especially useful if liquidity is an issue and so the speed of the return on investment is key.

2 One benefit of sensitivity analysis with investment appraisal is that it helps managers identify what might happen in different situations. This is useful for planning as it allows "what if" calculations and so managers can make better decisions.

3 Some factors that might be considered if a business invests in new technology are:
- The initial costs, as this will affect the overall returns from the investment and it may or may not be possible to raise this money in the first place for the project to go ahead.
- The likely profits; this will depend on the expected revenues and costs.
- The impact on stakeholders, e.g. employees. This may be a non-financial factor but managers will want to consider the impact on morale and staff goodwill and the likelihood of industrial action such as strikes.

4 The non-financial factors to consider when relocating include the likelihood of staff wanting to relocate; if they don't then the business will need to consider recruiting in the new area and how easy or difficult this is. Managers will also want to consider the impact on the brand of the region – is this a region that has positive connotations for the business? A wine business based in France may have more brand appeal than one based in Wales, for example. A computer business in the silicon valley in the US may sound better than one in another part of the world. The impact on the brand may be considered therefore.

5 The risks that may be involved in a major investment into a new product include the risk that the product will not make it to a successful launch. A product begins with a new idea. This idea has to be developed into a concept. This has to be tested and modified. This then has to be trialled and customer reaction assessed. Then it is launched. At any stage things can go wrong and the product may fail; even when launched competitors may take action to reduce the sales of your product. There is therefore a major financial risk. There is also a reputational risk if it fails. It may suggest that your management skills are lacking and that the business expertise in new product development is weak if a product fails.

Evaluation

6 Payback measures the time taken to repay initial investment. This is particularly useful if you are concerned about liquidity because you will want to know when you will get the investment back, and ideally this will be relatively quick. However, this method does not take an overview of total net inflows. It calculates when the initial investment is returned and ignores everything after that. The ARR is better in the sense that it takes an overview of the whole project and provides a profitability measure which can be compared with costs of borrowing and rates of return elsewhere.

Ideally, managers will look at both methods of investment appraisal as they provide different information. The relative importance of a method depends on the key factors for that business, e.g. can it afford to wait for the returns or does it need to be repaid relatively quickly?

7 Sensitivity analysis allows the business to assess an investment in different situations – for example, if costs were 2% higher than initially expected, if revenues were 3% higher, etc. This enables managers to assess the risk. Investment decisions are based on expectations and so it makes sense to assess a number of situations and consider the likelihood of different ones occurring. Thinking about the probabilities of different situations and the impact on the investment seems sensible.

However, managers cannot assess every possible situation and so they need to think what is most likely and focus on that. Whatever sensitivity analysis they do, they are still dealing with expectations rather than "knowns" and so there remains a risk. Also, whatever investment decision they make they still have to implement the decision effectively to try and ensure the planned returns are met. This means hitting sales targets and controlling costs.

In principle, sensitivity analysis is sensible, but the time taken to do it needs to be considered and managers need to be aware that risks still exist.

Chapter 8 – case studies, progress questions, exam-style questions

Case studies

Sonder

1 Other market penetration strategies are ways of increasing sales to existing customers with existing products. This could be achieved by changing elements of the marketing mix, e.g. cut prices to get customers to switch from existing providers, promote more to raise awareness or look for new distribution channels to find new ways of getting products to customers.

2 New product development involves developing a new product for existing customers. This is appealing because you know the customers already and so understand their needs. The risk is investing in developing a new product – many new products fail at some stage in the development process or even once launched. Diversification occurs when a business has new products aimed at new customers. This has a lot of risks because so much is new. However, it may be appealing if the business needs to target a new customer group (e.g. if the existing group is shrinking in size).

Which one is better depends on whether the existing market is big enough and potentially profitable enough. It also depends on how much research has been done and how much is known of the new customers. In both cases new products are developed, but the key is for whom – existing customers or new ones? This depends on the appeal of these segments – in terms of size, growth and profitability, but also the fit with the business strengths and risks.

Competition in the market for streaming

1 The strategies of Netflix and HBO have differed. Netflix has focused on developing new content. HBO has been more focused on short-term profit and maximising profit from existing content or content provided by others.

2 HBO might have changed its strategy because of the success of Netflix and the future threat it poses. If Netflix is growing in appeal then in the long term HBO may face a loss of sales and profits. It may be surviving in the short term by generating the returns it can out of its existing assets, but its long-term worries will be about Netflix's approach of generating content being more appealing to customers. Learning from Netflix, HBO has to respond to changing conditions.

3 Netflix and HBO have been following different strategies but Netflix has been winning market share with its approach of developing new content. This seems to have worried HBO and led it to want to respond by developing more of its own content as well. Developing new content seems to be effective at the moment for Netflix, but this will depend on the content generated. It is not just the volume of content that will matter but the nature and quality if it. It will be important to generate content that fits with customers, not just content for content's sake. Also, if others adopt a similar approach, the volume and quality of content may rise, making it more difficult to compete in this way – there may simply be too much good content and therefore the returns on any one programme may be low. New competitive advantages may emerge, especially with technological development.

Coffee wars

1 Coca-Cola has moved into a new market with a new product. This is known as diversification.

2 Coca-Cola has bought Costa because it wants a new income stream. The sales from its existing cola products are unlikely to rise rapidly with customer trends away from this type of drink. Coffee shops, by comparison, are doing well and sales are growing fast in different countries. Coca-Cola has many strengths and much expertise. It will want to bring its competences (such as marketing expertise) to Costa to add value.

3 The Ansoff matrix sets out strategic options. It considers products and markets in terms of whether they are existing or new. Its sets out four strategic options: market penetration, market development, new product development and diversification.

Using the Ansoff matrix can help to analyse strategic options and can help managers to think about issues such as risk. Managers can identify the type of strategy they are undertaking or considering and analyse the issues involved, such as the degree of risk or the fit with other strategies being pursued. However, ultimately it is just a planning tool. It can identify existing or future actions but it simply plots where strategies are. Managers must decide on which strategies are needed for the future and then implement them effectively. Using Ansoff can help to analyse a situation; that does not guarantee success but may help it. Many managers say the real challenge is not identifying the right strategy but making it actually work.

Progress questions

1 • A business invests in more promotional activities to increase sales of its existing products to its existing customers: this is market penetration.
   • A business develops a new range of products for its existing customers: this is new product development.
   • A business starts to sell its existing products in new overseas markets: this is market development.
   • A business develops a new product to target a market segment that is new to it: this is diversification.

2 Risk is the probability that something will harm the business.

3 An Ansoff matrix shows possible strategic options in terms of markets and products.

4 Market penetration means selling more existing products in existing markets.

5 Market development means selling more existing products in new markets.

6 New product development means selling new products in existing markets.

7 Diversification means selling new products in new markets.

8 The labels of the Ansoff matrix are: new and existing products; new and existing markets.

9 A product that is expensive can still be competitive if it offers sufficient benefits to justify the high price.

10 The axes of Bowman's clock show: price relative to rivals; benefits relative to rivals.

11 Strategic positioning is the price-benefit combination offered by the business, e.g. low benefit–low price or high benefit–high price.

12 Competitive advantage is the ability to offer a better, more compelling combination of price and benefits relative to rivals.

13 Differentiation means offering distinctive benefits compared to those of rivals – for which the business may be able to charge more.

Exam-style questions

Explanation and analysis

1 One benefit of a market penetration strategy compared to a market development strategy is that the business is focusing on a market it knows; this means it has more experience and established networks and this may reduce risk.

2 One benefit of a diversification strategy compared to a market penetration strategy is that the business is operating in a new market with a new product; this may offer more opportunities for growth than in a declining market with sales of existing products falling.

3 Two factors that might influence the strategic positioning of a business are as follows. The positioning of rivals – for example, you may want to compete in a different segment rather than attack an existing business head on. The profitability of different options will also be important – this is because investors and managers will be looking for a certain rate of return on any project.

4 A business may change its strategy if its existing strategy is failing; if sales and profits are falling, for example, there will be pressure to consider what can be done and whether a different strategy (e.g. competing in a different market or with different products) could work. A business may also reconsider its strategy if the opportunities and threats have changed. For example, changes in the economy or the political situation may make some markets more appealing than they were and other ones far less attractive.

5 Maintaining a competitive advantage will be difficult because rivals will want to imitate it so they have the benefits as well. This means that there will be constant imitation and innovation to copy or surpass what you do. It may be possible to protect in the short term, e.g. legal protection such as a patent, but if you are making high profits rivals will try to find ways around any barriers (e.g. by developing a similar product but one that does not break the patent). Patents will eventually run out anyway and then anyone can imitate the product directly. Business is competitive and businesses try to learn from each other and ensure they do not fall behind.

Evaluation

6 A market penetration strategy involves existing products and existing markets; in some ways this is low risk because the business knows both the market and products. A new product development strategy involves a new product in an existing market. This may revitalise a market and generate high sales and fast growth. However, there is the risk taken developing a new product; many new products fail at some stage of the development or launch process.

Which of the two strategies is better depends on:
   • Market growth opportunities within existing markets with existing products; if these opportunities are high, penetration may be the better and safer option.
   • The likely success of new product development – what resources does the business have? What skills? How good at product development is it?
   • Both are potentially good strategies and can be carried out at the same time. Whether one is better than the other depends on how good the business is at them, market conditions, rivals' actions and what the business is trying to achieve.

7 A diversification strategy involves new products and new markets. This has risk as so much is unknown and the managers lack experience and insight into these areas. However, the appeal of this strategy is that it moves the business out of existing markets and products which may be mature products or in declining markets. Getting out of the existing products and markets may actually reduce the risk of staying with them.

How risky diversification is depends on:

- How new the new product is and your capabilities in this area.
- How new the market is and your experience of this type of market.
- How risky it may be not to do this and stay with existing products in existing markets.
- How it is approached, e.g. what research is done and how plans are produced and implemented.

Diversification needs to be managed carefully to control the risks of developing new products and entering new markets.

Chapter 9 – case studies, progress questions, exam-style questions

Case studies

Innocent

1 Two factors that might influence the price paid for Innocent include the value of the brand – Coca-Cola will consider what they could do with the brand, e.g. to launch more products under this name. Coca-Cola will also value other assets such as land, inventory and cash that Innocent holds. Coca-Cola will also look to the future and consider what products are about to be launched and what the future market conditions might be, as this will affect the likely profitability of the business and therefore how much could be paid for it.

2 The three founders of Innocent sold the business because they wanted to move on eventually and turn all their hard work into cash. They had worked in the business for many years and built up the business. By selling their shares they can turn this effort into money. Also the business at that stage was short of funds; the sale gave the individuals personally and the business as a whole the funds they needed and wanted.

3 Innocent had been developed and managed by three people since it started. They had always had strong ethical values and this had been a key feature of the way they operated and how and what they produced. Ethics were an integral part of the brand. For example, money was given to charity and products were not transported too far because of the environmental impact. Ethics therefore were important to the individuals and the brand and would be one factor the owners considered when selling the business. They would have wanted reassurances on how the business would develop under Coca-Cola.

However the relative importance of this depends on:

- Why they sold – were their motives purely financial?
- How much they needed the money.
- Who else they could have sold to; they may have had few options and therefore would not have been in a strong bargaining position.

McDonald's

1 Buying a McDonald's franchise appeals in many ways. It brings a global brand and a huge amount of expertise. It gives access to products and processes.

Franchisees are given systems rather than having to develop them themselves. All of this means the risks are lower and it is easier to run a business within set rules and ways of doing things.

However, there are initial costs to buy the franchises (as well as a selection process) and ongoing costs which have to be paid to McDonald's. There are also restrictions on what you can and cannot do as a franchisee.

Ultimately it depends on:

- The precise terms and conditions relative to your expected returns.
- The opportunity costs – what else can you do?
- How much you want the freedom to decide what to do and how to do it.
- The success of the McDonald's brand at the time.
- The performance and quality of other franchisees, as you will be dependent on their success and behaviour as you are linked though the brand name.

GlaxoSmithKline

1 A joint venture might lead to a reduction in costs for the businesses involved because they can share resources and expertise. They won't need to duplicate some activities, such as research facilities, which can reduce costs.

2 GlaxoSmithKline might want to split its businesses to enable each business unit to focus on its own priorities. This might give greater clarity for managers and enable better decision making. Splitting up the businesses may help it to avoid diseconomies of scale; it can avoid

some of the control, communication and coordination problems that large-scale businesses can experience. Being smaller can allow better communication and give greater responsiveness and autonomy for each business according to its own conditions.

3 A merger occurs when two or more businesses join together to become one business. A joint venture occurs where businesses cooperates on a particular project. A joint venture may avoid some of the culture clashes that can occur with mergers because the businesses are not fully uniting; this can avoid conflict. A joint venture may also avoid some diseconomies of scale because the business as a whole is not getting as big as it would with a merger. This can avoid some of the communication and control problems that can lead to higher unit costs. A joint venture may also enable a business to share resources and expertise where it adds value without having to come together where synergies do not exist.

However, a full merger may provide greater economies of scale and greater market power. It could lead to purchasing, managerial and technical economies leading to lower unit costs. This can improve profits.

Ultimately, it depends on the terms and conditions of the joint venture in terms of how well it works. It depends on the benefits of collaborating and the relative impact on economies and diseconomies of scale. A joint venture may be a good first step to try out whether a merger might work.

Spotify

1 Artists who produce music will want to earn their returns from the sales of their music. They want a fee every time their music is played. They also want to make sure no one copies their music and this is why copyright is important. There would be little incentive to produce music if it could be immediately copied. Copyright means the creator of the music can sell the right for others to use it; for example, for adverts. This helps to increase the earnings of music creators and encourages people to be musicians.

Innovation at Tata

1 A conglomerate owns different types of business. This helps reduce the risk of being in business. If sales in one market decline the business has other products and so overall sales may not fall that much. Being a conglomerate spreads risks.

2 Innovation involves creating new products and processes. New processes allow Tata to produce more efficiently (for example with new technology) and perhaps offer a better customer service (for example with online ordering). Innovation in terms of products enables Tata to offer new improved products and retain and attract customers. Innovation can therefore be good for revenue and for costs and can increase the profitability of Tata.

3 More investment provides the funds that may be necessary for research and development and to pay for the scientific research that can lead to innovation. More money can pay for better staff with more skills and experience, and this may help with new ideas and better follow through on ideas. This can help innovation. More money may also help schemes such as kaizen schemes to encourage more ideas and new ways of doing things.

However, more money may not be enough. Money may be wasted. It may be used on the wrong things or just used badly. The success of investment into innovation centres will depend on who has the money, how it is used and how well managed the investments are. There is always an element of risk investing in innovation but these risks can be reduced with the right people and systems.

Merlin

1 Demand for visitor attractions will depend on the quality of the attraction itself; the rides, the activities for people to do when there and the quality of accommodation will affect the appeal and how much people want to come. Transport facilities and the infrastructure also count because they affect how easy it is to get there; the easier it is to get there, the bigger the catchment area and the higher demand may be.

2 Having a portfolio of products means the business is reducing its risk. This is because a decrease in demand for one product may be offset by an increase in demand for another. This can lead to more stable earnings and therefore more stable rewards for investors; this might help the business be more attractive to investors, boosting demand for shares and share price and making the company worth more.

3 China may be a good market for Peppa Pig if it has sufficient people of the right age with an interest in the brand and with the income required for a theme park. Obviously China has a huge potential market which is appealing, but Merlin needs to understand the culture well to be sure that this theme park will attract customers. A great deal will depend on what is actually offered and how this fits needs and where the park is based – it needs to be accessible to a big market. It will depend on the effectiveness of the marketing to promote the business and on factors such as the pricing. China has the

potential to generate good returns, but it depends on what is offered and how well the offering is executed.

Smartphones

1 There are many different parts in a smartphone and there are very high levels of competition. Manufacturers will look all over the world to find the best components at the lowest prices. To do this they will then manage the logistics of dealing with suppliers everywhere which is why there is a global supply chain.

2 Managing a global supply chain brings many challenges. Managers will have to coordinate the transport and delivery of products across borders, which may be difficult in terms of the transportation and also in terms of the regulations and paperwork needed to move products around the world. There are always potential disruptions, such as the weather, political disagreements halting imports or exports, or natural disasters. Managers may be organising orders from lots of countries throughout the day and this brings the challenges of communication and synchronising the actions required.

3 To be competitive a business must offer better value for money than its rivals. To do this requires the right combination of benefits and price. Operating internationally allows a business to access the very best in the world – such as designers, resources, skills and facilities. By looking globally you can see what others are doing and you can access what you need at the best price and quality. If you only focus nationally you are restricting your choices and therefore your ability to compete. However, operating internationally is not easy – you need expertise and resources which may not be available to everyone. Not every business will know how to find the best suppliers, how to work with them and how to manage them. So although being international may help a business compete, this will only happen if it is done well, which will not always be the case.

VW in Rwanda

1 Nigeria might want to protect its domestic car manufacturers by imposing tariffs or quotas on foreign producers to reduce the number coming in to the country or increasing their prices with a tax. This should help the Nigerian car producers to survive and lead to more employment.

2 VW is opening up in Rwanda because it is an emerging economy. At the moment demand may be relatively low because the population has a low average income. However, although the profit may be low on each item, it may create high profits if enough are sold. More importantly, it may help to promote the brand name and raise its profile. It will help to establish the dealership network. This may be useful if the economy grows and incomes rise. VW may be in a good position then to exploit this opportunity and achieve higher sales and profits in the future.

3 Payback measures the length of time an investment takes to repay the initial investment. The average rate of return measures the average profit per year as a percentage of the initial investment. When entering the Rwandan market VW almost certainly thinks this is a long-term project. In the short term the business will probably not make high profits. Customers do not have high incomes and VW may not have high earnings at first. However, if it establishes itself and the brand it can be present as the market grows. Over time incomes will increase and VW will be able to sell higher-value cars at higher prices. VW will therefore probably not expect a quick payback but will hope for a good average return over a long period of time.

Ikea

1 Ikea will consider the likely demand for its products because it determines revenue and returns on investment. The demand will depend on the population size in the appropriate age ranges, their income levels and their tastes in furniture and furnishings. Managers will also consider the regulations and laws in the country because this will affect how easy it is to set up, how easy it is to operate and the ease of competing. If the laws are complex and it is difficult to meet the various standards and regulations this may deter Ikea from setting up in India.

2 The problems of operating in India may include cultural differences. Ikea will need to understand the Indian culture because this will affect how people buy, the level and nature of service they expect, and how and where to promote its products. Indian culture may be very different from Swedish or European cultures and this will affect all aspects of doing business, including managing people; it is important to understand what drives people and how they should be treated.

3 Selling overseas allows businesses to access more customers. They have access potentially to billions of customers. This can boost sales and lead to more profits. It can also reduce the risk of being dependent on one market. This can make overseas expansion very attractive. However, there are significant risks. You may not understand how to do business in this new market with different regulations, a different economic environment and different cultures.

This can mean the decisions made are wrong and mistakes are made. You are not operating in familiar territory. You may not have the right experience, expertise or networks. All of this means failure may be more likely overseas.

This means you have to be careful to choose the right markets, the right way of entering at the right time. Success will not be guaranteed.

Greek shipping

1 One country may ban trade with another to put pressure on it to change its politics; for example, a government may want another government to stop nuclear testing and therefore ban imports from the other country to exert economic pressure for change.

2 The ban on Iranian oil will affect the movement of this oil around the world and therefore this is likely to reduce demand for Greek shipping companies. The falling demand will reduce revenue and profits. The Greek companies are likely to have excess capacity and may even consider not using some of their vessels or not repairing vessels if broken. However, demand for oil is likely to increase and this presumably will mean more demand for Greek shipping (assuming they win the contracts) which will compensate for the loss of Iranian oil contracts.

3 If there are lost orders due to the loss of Iranian contracts this is likely to lead to less sales and profits for Greek shipping companies. This is likely to lead to fewer rewards for investors as dividends may fall and the share price may fall (due to less demand for the companies' shares). If demand is not replaced from other contracts, fewer staff may be needed because the work is not there and so employees may suffer. Managers will be under pressure to find ways of compensating for the lost orders; for example managers might seek cost cuts through redundancies. Suppliers to the shipping companies will also suffer because there will be less work for them and less money for them because the shipping companies will be cost conscious. Overall, because the loss of contracts is bad for the shipping companies this is likely to be bad for all stakeholders – there will be fewer orders, less money and less demand for people and resources.

Progress questions

1 Organic growth is internal growth; the business sells more of its products. External growth occurs when a business acquires another business.

2 Economies of scale occur when unit costs fall as the business expands. Diseconomies of scale occur when unit costs rise as the business expands.

3 Backward vertical integration involves buying suppliers. This might improve the competitiveness of a business by gaining control of suppliers. This may reduce costs and may give greater control over quality.

4 Horizontal integration involves buying another business at the same stage of the same production process. This might improve the competitiveness of a business by leading to economies of scale and reducing unit costs. This type of integration also reduces rivalry, which should increase the market power of the business.

5 Intrapreneurship occurs when people within the business are entrepreneurial.

6 Two reasons for selling abroad are: to access more customers; and to reduce the risk of being dependent on the domestic market.

7 Protectionism occurs when a government protects its businesses against foreign competition – for example through tariffs and quotas.

Exam-style questions

Explanation and analysis questions

1 One benefit of organic growth compared to external growth is that there is less danger of culture clash because two separate businesses are not involved; the culture of the original business can be maintained more easily as it is growing itself.

2 Protectionism such as tariffs and quotas against overseas businesses may help local businesses with more demand. Overseas businesses may be taxed, making them more expensive and less competitive, meaning local businesses experience an increase in demand. Or overseas businesses may face a quota so there is a limit on the number and customers have to buy from local businesses. Again demand increases.

3 A business may struggle to be innovative because its staff may lack the skills, attitude or motivation to innovate. Even if the funds were available the employees may not be able to use these effectively to generate better ideas for products or processes. At the same time, funds may be difficult to get hold of; the business may not have the funds or be available to borrow to finance innovation.

4 A manufacturer may look at the likely market size to decide whether to target or not. The business will want enough demand to generate the revenue and profit required to justify the investment; managers will want sufficient return on investment. Managers may also look

at the degree of competition and how competitors might react if they targeted this country. If the competitors cut prices to undercut the new entrant this might reduce the likely profits and make the returns so low that it is not worth competing.

5   Using Greiner's model of growth a business will face a variety of crises as it grows over time. The nature of the crisis will depend on which stage the business is at. For example, it may involve the need for more leadership in the early years, the need for more independence by different business units if control mechanisms have become too tight, or the need for more coordination if the organisation is operating in many business areas. Often solving one problem then leads to another. For example, imposing control to manage growth may then lead to too little independence of different business units.

Evaluation questions

6   A franchise occurs when one business sells the right to its name and product to another business. Buying a franchise may provide a trusted and proven business model, saving time on building a brand and reducing the risk because the product has an established track record. The franchisor may also provide training and useful market research.

However, a franchise will usually involve an initial cost and will involve sacrificing a percentage of revenue. It also involves risks because you may be vulnerable to actions of other franchisees – if they make mistakes or have bad press coverage this will affect the other franchisees as they share the same brand name.

Whether to buy a franchise or not depends on the franchisor – for example, how strong the brand is, how good the support provided is and what the charges are. In theory, a franchise reduces risks because there is so much information that exists and support is available. However, it does tie you in to the franchisor and if there are problems with other franchisees you can suffer as well, so risks still exist.

7   Moving offshore may enable a shoe manufacturer to benefit from lower labour costs because of cheaper labour in some countries. It may also benefit from lower land costs and lower material costs. All of this may mean lower costs and higher profitability; moving offshore may increase the return on investment. There may be other reasons for moving offshore – there may be particular skills or expertise available which is not available locally.

Offshore production can therefore bring quality and/or cost benefits. These provide reasons for relocating.

However, there are also challenges with offshoring. There can be challenges ensuring that quality does not suffer because it may be more difficult to manage overseas. There may be communication problems and there may be delays with products arriving back in the domestic market due to transportation issues.

Overall, offshoring cannot be guaranteed to be a good thing. It depends on the costs and quality benefits relative to the potential complexity and challenges of managing a business overseas.

Chapter 10 – case studies, progress questions, exam-style questions

Case studies

Apple

1   Jobs brought expertise to the position that allowed him to make better decisions than others and ensure the business chose the right strategy, and this helped ensure it met its objectives. His expertise meant fewer mistakes were made and fewer resources were wasted. He also brought a vision, which means he looked ahead and ensured the business kept innovating and kept developing new products and new business processes; this helped to ensure it remained competitive.

2   Someone like Jobs can inspire others. People wanted to work for him, he helped to attract the best talent and ensured commitment and alignment from everyone. People like him can think outside the box and therefore can be innovative and help the business remain competitive. They can make change happen in the business because they are followed and listened. They can look ahead and have the vision to provide a strategy for the future.

However, leaders need others to help make it happen; they can inspire others but it does require others to implement the decisions made. Success cannot happen just because of the leader; the leader needs supporters and help.

Leaders also need resources – they need the finance and the equipment and land to bring about successful change and a successful strategy.

Success will also depend on external factors such as the economy and political and social factors. For example, the actions of rivals will affect the success of a business.

So Jobs clearly played a key role; however, even without him the business can flourish, so it is not necessarily all down to one person.

PepsiCo

1   PepsiCo has appointed a new leader from the inside because it knows the person's track record, which may reduce risk. This appointment suggests there is room to be promoted within the business, which can be motivating and may make staff stay at the business. The person will know the culture of the business already, which will reduce induction training and reduce the risk of them leaving because they don't like the culture.

2   A leader can:
   • Set out the vision and strategy; the strategy is key to achievement of objectives.
   • Inspire and motivate staff, which can attract and retain the very best people.
   • Look ahead to where the business should be rather than focus on where it is, which ensures the business moves forward and remains competitive.

If a leader gets it wrong the strategy can be wrong or it can be badly implemented and the business can fail.

However, the success or failure of a business also depends on other factors such as:
   • The external environment; success is less likely if the target markets are declining due to poor economic growth or if markets are being closed due to trade disputes.
   • Rivals; for example, if they are developing new and better products than yours.
   • The resources of the business; for example, a lack of finance may prevent investment in essential technology.

A leader is an important factor but he/she does not control all the factors that influence the success of a business.

Deutsche Bank

1   The new Chief Executive brought about these changes at Deutsche Bank because he needed to cut costs. The company was making a loss and its share price was falling. The Chief Executive needed to be seen to act and find ways of improving the profitability of the business. One way is to cut costs and if he thinks this can be done by losing staff without affecting the quality of service and customer experience (perhaps due to greater technology) this may be the best way of achieving better performance.

2   The best way of bringing about these changes depends on the timeline and the costs and benefits involved. It is a good idea to involve staff to identify how the changes can be made. Staff may have ideas about how it can be done better and less painfully. It may be better to have the cooperation and understanding of staff when making redundancies. It may be important (and a legal requirement in some countries) to involve staff. This may well include education to explain why the changes are being made. Negotiating may be possible if employees can provide enough benefits to justify any concessions. However, the Chief Executive may not be able to give too many concessions because of the changes that have to be made. The Chief Executive has to do something and so may only be able to negotiate provided the same overall costs savings are made.

Shell's scenario planning

1   The benefits to a business such as Shell of scenario planning are that the business looks far ahead at where the market it is in is going and anticipates various scenarios. It can then plan how it would be competitive in that scenario and start to organise the resources and strategy to do so if needed. It helps to ensure managers are in control of the business and where it is headed rather than having to react to what has happened. Scenario planning is part of the process of investigating the external environment to identify relevant opportunities and threats and plan accordingly.

2   Scenario planning helps a business look ahead and consider the business environment in the future. This helps the business to be ready for possible situations and have the resources and strategy in place to maximise performance in these conditions. It is long-term planning, looking for significant shifts in the business environment which will involve extensive planning over many years. For a bank, the Chief Executive might want to consider what the world of banking will look like ten or twenty years from now – what are the fundamental changes that might occur? She or he might be interested in the global economy in the future – where will the growth come from? What will be the most powerful financial nations? Scenario planning therefore makes sense when you want a big picture of what the world might look like, and this may be sensible for the Chief Executive of a global bank. However, she or he will want to determine how much to spend on this, who to involve and how many scenarios to work on to ensure the returns justify this activity. She or he cannot

invest limitless amounts of money so needs to decide the level of investment that justifies it. So yes, invest, but decide how much is justified given the other demands of the business.

Amazon's culture

1. Amazon wants its employees to be "customer centric" so that they focus on making sure the customer experience is the best it can be. By doing this the business meets the needs of its customers and it is the business they choose.

2. Amazon wants a culture where employees take risks because it wants innovation. It does not mind if some ideas do not work as long as the ones that do compensate for the ones that don't. It wants people to try things because that is what leads to innovation and creativity.

3. To create a culture that encourages employees to take risks Amazon might reward those who do take risks, so it is shown this is a good thing to do. It might promote risk takers, again sending the message that this is desirable. It can ensure funds are available for people to develop their ideas and the structure is not too formal or fixed. It will not pay to praise, promote or reward those who do not take risks.

The China–Pakistan Economic Corridor

1. Network analysis could help businesses involved in the construction of the China–Pakistan Economic Corridor by getting experts to identify the tasks involved and what order they can be undertaken. By setting out a network analysis managers can identify the critical activities, to ensure the project is completed as fast as possible, the float time on other activities, and the earliest start and latest finish times. This can help plan when materials are required and ensure everyone is alert to deadlines and target times. Network analysis is therefore a valuable planning tool for a project as complex and significant as this. It will help coordinate the activities of many different contractors. It will also be used to identify how serious any delays are by considering the float time if there is any.

Progress questions

1. A leader is someone with followers who has a vision of where to go next.

2. The sources of power of a leader include expert power, resources power, personal power.

3. A sell style of leadership is where a leader explains the idea to employees and "sells" its benefits to get them to support it.

4. A consultative style of leadership is where a leader seeks the advice and ideas of employees before making the decision; he/she consults with subordinates.

5. The success of a leader may depend on his or her previous experience, how much support he or she gets from the directors, the resources he or she has at his or her disposal and the support from other employees.

6. The influences on the style of leadership may include the ability of employees; the nature of the task; what has worked in the past.

7. The success of a leader in bringing about a change in strategy might be affected by the acceptance by employees, the resources available, the style adopted, and whether the strategy is right for the business and its circumstances.

8. Incremental change happens slowly; it happens in small stages over time. Disruptive change occurs when there is a dramatic change that alters the way a market operates.

9. An organic structure is flexible and involves teams being created as and when needed. A mechanistic structure has set rules and procedures, with people having a clear role in the organisation.

10. A mechanistic structure may be more appropriate than an organic one if managers want set outcomes. If they want to be sure how jobs are being done, who does what, how they do it, who reports to who and what the outcomes look like then a mechanistic structure is ideal.

11. Drivers for change are factors that bring about change – for example a decline in sales or a new manager. Forces resisting change are those factors making change less likely, such as staff who are reluctant to change or a lack of funds to finance change.

12. Employees may resist change because they are worried they will be worse off, they prefer things as they are or they don't understand why change is necessary.

13. To overcome resistance to change, managers may explain the reasons why it is happening; they may offer incentives to staff who change; or they may simply force change through by telling people they have to do it.

14. Contingency planning occurs when managers plan for unlikely situations that could cause a risk to the business.

15. The culture of a well-established business will be determined by the reward systems. People will believe in the business and behave in a way that gets them rewards. Whatever people are given bonuses for or promoted for will signal that this is what the business values

and will move the culture towards this. Even if the business is well established, the founders, values may still matter; this is because people will have been recruited over the years and they may have been chosen based on how much they agree with the founders' principles. In some businesses the founder's story and values are regularly retold to affect the current culture.

16. A long-term rather than short-term culture may lead to more investment in training, in research and development, and brand building. Projects that have a high return but long payback may be more likely to be undertaken.

17. In a group culture the rewards would be linked to the performance of the whole team. Commission, for example, would be divided between the team. In a more individual culture rewards would be paid to the best individual performing salesperson or employee.

18. To change the culture of a business, managers may change the reward systems to reward new behaviours. They may promote the people who do what they want and not promote people who don't. Managers may train staff in the new key values and make these values visible in stories and press coverage about the business to show they matter.

19. A strategy is a long-term plan to achieve the objectives of the business.

20. The benefit of strategic planning is that it helps to ensure that what you are doing is appropriate to the business environment. You will examine the strengths and weaknesses of the present position and the opportunities and threats in the external environment to produce a plan that helps the objectives to be achieved. It will help managers to allocate resources efficiently and effectively and to ensure everyone is working towards the same targets, and to communicate and coordinate activities.

21. A functional organisational structure means that jobs are organised and grouped according to their function; for example, all of the marketing jobs, the finance jobs and operations jobs are grouped in particular departments.

    The advantages of this approach are that people with similar skills and working in the same area can share their experiences and insights. This can lead to better functional decision making. However, the potential disadvantage is the "silo effect" whereby the marketing team do not consider an issue from an HR or operations or finance perspective. People can become too focused on a single objective and not see the entire perspective on a situation. This can worsen decision making.

22. A leader can inspire employees and gain their commitment. This can lead employees to be aligned with the strategy and work efficiently and effectively towards it. The leader can ensure resources are available in the right places to make the strategy work, and make sure the returns are sufficient. The leader can make sure the business has the right people in the right places. This means they have the skills, experience and expertise to make the right decisions to make the strategy work. A leader has to work through others and so has to have the right team around him or her.

23. Good communication is important to the success of a strategy because a strategy is a plan. To work, everyone involved in the plan must know what they are doing, how it interrelates with others, what resources they have and how success is judged. Good communication is essential to the success of a strategy because it is needed to set out the targets, the methods to achieve these that can be used, the standards and ethics to be adopted and to measure how well the strategy is doing.

24. An organisational structure sets out the way jobs are organised and the reporting relationships within an organisation. It determines who does what, who else they work with, who they report to. The design of this structure should be to complement the strategy. If you operate in very different regional markets, for example, then you might design a structure that is regional; this way jobs are grouped around a particular part of the world, providing a specific focus on the demands and needs of this region. If, however, the key difference was not the regions you operated in but the products you made (perhaps you make food and cosmetics, for example) these will have very different requirements in terms of marketing and operations, and so a product structure might make more sense. The structure will affect the focus and the efficiency of decision making and needs to support the strategy.

25. Float times
    A 12 − 5 − 2 = 5 days
    B 1 day
    C 0 days
    D 7 days

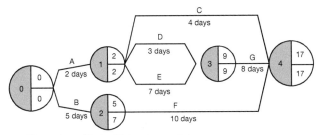

The project will take 17 days to complete.

The critical path is AEG.

27 Strategic drift occurs when a strategy fails to change in line with changes in the external environment; the strategy is no longer appropriate.

28 Strategic drift occurs because managers fail to see what is happening around them; this may be because they are not looking, or they don't interpret the data properly or they fail to take action.

29 A business can avoid strategic drift by keeping alert to what is happening around them; this means undertaking market research where appropriate and talking to experts in the field to keep alert to change. Managers need to build a culture that is open to change and a structure and workforce that is flexible to change.

Exam-style questions

Explanation and analysis

1 One factor that would make a "consult" style of leadership appropriate is if employees had expertise and experience that would be useful to use. You might consult if you need employees, understanding and agreement.

2 Managers of an airline might benefit from contingency planning by trying to anticipate what might happen and being ready for this. For example, they might plan for an emergency landing and ensure that everyone is fully trained for this to ensure the negative consequences are minimised.

3 The culture in countries could vary by being short term vs long term; in some countries the focus will be on short-term results whereas in others there may be greater willingness to invest in projects that bring longer-term resources. Some societies are very hierarchical and there will be a clear hierarchy in the business; in other countries the value of someone will depend on what they can bring to a project rather than their job title and position.

4 Network analysis can be used to identify the quickest way to complete a project given the level of resources and the level of quality required. If you organising activities appropriately (e.g. with some activities running in parallel wherever possible) you can speed up the development of a product or the completion of a project. If a product can be launched more quickly the payback period (how long it takes to repay the initial investment) is quicker. Using network analysis also means managers can order materials just when they are needed rather than too early. This means that money won't be wasted on storage or supplies that have to be thrown away because they have deteriorated over time. Reducing costs improves profitability and can reduce the payback time for an investment project.

5 People resist change for various reasons, such as preferring the way things are, disagreeing with the way the change is being done or the nature of the change, or not understanding why the change is occurring in the first place. New contracts will often cause some resistance as people may feel they are unfair or they are worse off than others or than they were.

Whether to find a compromise or force it through depends on how important it is to keep the changes the way they are. The Chief Executive will consider the costs and impact of compromise; it may not be affordable or possible to make any changes. The effects of not changing will also be considered. How serious is the resistance? What action will employees take? How many employees are involved? What are the risks and costs of employees' resistance? The Chief Executive will need to weigh up the dangers of not changing with the dangers of changing these contracts to decide whether or not a compromise is possible or whether the change just needs to be forced through.

Evaluation

6 If profits are falling the owners may want to replace the Chief Executive because she or he is not generating the rewards they need and expect. Owners usually invest in a business to gain from the value of the business growing and payments from profits. However, whether the Chief Executive can be replaced depends on what the cause of the falling profits is; is it due to poor leadership or is it external factors? Are profits falling but still relatively good in the circumstances, or are they disappointing generally?

The leader can have a big impact on performance but there are other factors; it may be that removing the leader makes the position worse not better. Changing the Chief Executive may upset staff, may lead to conflict elsewhere and may lead to a power vacuum if a good new Chief Executive cannot be found.

7 In a functional structure the jobs are grouped by functions such as marketing, operations, human resources and finance. A benefit of this is that the specialist functional areas work together. The marketing team can share marketing skills and resources; the HR team can share their policies and experiences. However, the danger of a functional structure is that it can lead to a silo approach whereby the different functions do not share ideas, resources and insights across the functions.

A matrix structure involves individuals having two or more managers. For example, someone working on the UK Ford Mondeo may report to the global model manager who has insight into Mondeo globally and the UK Ford manager who has an insight into all Ford products in the UK. This means there are different perspectives. The danger is that an individual may get conflicting instructions and not know who to follow.

In the case of multinational companies with many products, the best solution may be a matrix. This is because individuals can benefit from the perspective of different countries and different products, and bring these experiences together. This can lead to better decision making, learning from different products and different countries. However, it will require everyone to be clear about what to do when instructions conflict. Given the variety of products and countries, the demands on the different functions will vary considerably and the matrix structure may help cope with this.

Index

Page numbers in **bold** indicate key terms boxes.